EFFECTIVE
FIRST-PERSON
BIBLICAL
PREACHING

D0171202

EFFECTIVE
FIRST-PERSON
BIBLICAL
PREACHING

The Steps
from Text
to Narrative
Sermon

J. KENT EDWARDS

GRAND RAPIDS, MICHIGAN 49530 USA

ZONDERVAN™

Effective First-Person Biblical Preaching
Copyright © 2005 by J. Kent Edwards

Requests for information should be addressed to:
Zondervan, *Grand Rapids, Michigan 49530*

Library of Congress Cataloging-in-Publication Data

Edwards, J. Kent, 1958–.
    Effective first-person biblical preaching : the steps from text to narrative
sermon / J. Kent Edwards.
       p. cm.
    Summary: "A practical resource to help students and pastors understand why and how
first-person sermons can be preached with biblical integrity. Includes extensive examples
and worksheets"—Provided by publisher.
    Includes bibliographical references and indexes
    ISBN-10: 0-310-26309-3 (hardcover)
    ISBN-13: 978-0-310-26309-8
    1. Narrative preaching. I. Title.
BV4235.S76 E39 2005
251—dc22
                                                             2005003954
                                                                     CIP

Individuals may make photocopies of the material on pp. 167–181 (in appendix 2) for personal
use or for classroom or seminar use, not to exceed one copy per attendee.

This edition printed on acid-free paper.

All Scripture quotations, unless otherwise indicated, are taken from the *Holy Bible: New Inter-national Version*®. NIV®. Copyright © 1973, 1978, 1984 by International Bible Society. Used by
permission of Zondervan. All rights reserved.

The website addresses recommended throughout this book are offered as a resource to you. These
websites are not intended in any way to be or imply an endorsement on the part of Zondervan,
nor do we vouch for their content for the life of this book.

All rights reserved. No part of this publication may be reproduced, stored in a retrieval system,
or transmitted in any form or by any means—electronic, mechanical, photocopy, recording, or
any other—except for brief quotations in printed reviews, without the prior permission of the
publisher.

Interior design by Sharon VanLoozenoord

Printed in the United States of America

05 06 07 08 09 10 11 /❖ DCI/ 15 14 13 12 11 10 9 8 7 6 5 4 3 2 1

To Nola
My wife. My love.

CONTENTS

FOREWORD

Over thirty years ago Ernest T. Campbell published a book of sermons with the unsettling title, *Locked in a Room with Open Doors*. If you think about that image, it can make your palms sweat and your nervous system shiver.

Millions of men and women, of course, are trapped in rooms with closed doors. They lack education or the ability to read. They feel comfortable where they are and have no interest or motivation to change. Opportunities open to others are simply not open to them. They do what they can with what they have.

It is something else, though, to be locked in a room with open doors. The most confining lock-in involves our refusal to handle new ways of thinking. We can be stuck in place when we feel we are justified by some practice rather than by faith. As a case in point, many evangelical ministers have been trained to study the Bible in seminary. They have a reverence for the text. Yet they transfer their strong allegiance to the Scriptures to some single approach to preparing sermons that they were taught.

Most seminary students have been prepared to preach by using the epistles, and as graduates they feel comfortable with that genre of literature. Then when they come to narrative, the most-used genre in the Bible, they either ignore it or read it as though this literature is another letter to be analyzed. Such ministers resemble the physician who was an expert at setting broken bones but wasn't prepared to deal with other maladies. When patients came to him complaining of a stomach ache or a high fever, he would break their bones so he could treat them. Lesson: All patients and all passages are not the same.

We may be locked in a room with open doors, therefore, when it comes to reading the biblical narratives for other reasons. Perhaps this ineptness can be traced to our childhood as well as our seminary training. If we think of biblical stories merely as bedtime tales to read to our children or as Sunday school illustrations from which to draw morals for good behavior, we will fail to read them as they really are: profound theology taught through stories. Or if we have approached the Old Testament writings only as illustrations of New Testament truth, we will be closed to the life-altering truths the inspired writers of the first testament communicated. There are basic techniques of the storyteller's art that can open the reader to the large sections of narrative in the Word of God. The obstacle to using them correctly may simply be our hesitancy to enter an open door.

In addition to understanding these narratives, there are also ways of presenting them so that listeners can hear them again for the first time. One of these approaches joins imagination to exegesis. The preacher retells a narrative from the vantage point of a character within the story. This joining brings both the left brain and the right brain into play. As a result hearers "see" what they might otherwise have missed had the preacher merely dissected the story like a schoolboy cutting up a frog. When that is done, the people get the parts but miss the life of the narrative.

In this book, Kent Edwards opens the doors to narrative literature and the first-person sermon. The reward for the reader is that they can find new freedom in their preaching.

Haddon Robinson
May 2005

WHAT I HAVE LEARNED
ALONG THE WAY

A cynic once defined preaching as "the fine art of speaking in someone else's sleep." The problem with cynics is that sometimes they are correct. Congregants repeatedly complain of falling asleep during their pastor's sermons. The unchurched choose to stay home Sunday mornings because they suspect what churchgoers already know: that it is more comfortable to sleep in a bed than in a pew.

I recently heard of a pastor in England who was determined to preach the longest sermon in history. His goal was to speak for at a minimum of thirty-six hours in order to earn his way into the *Guinness World Records* book. The pastor was hoping that his parishioners would sponsor his hourly efforts and that this extra income would keep the church open and his job secure. I never heard if the Reverend accomplished his goal, but I do think his energies would have been better spent trying to preach the world's most interesting sermon. People would give serious money to hear that kind of a message!

The only thing worse than listening to long, boring sermons is knowing that you are preaching one of them. It is a terrible experience to stand behind the pulpit on a beautiful Sunday morning and watch eyes glaze over and heads begin to nod. You don't want to put people to sleep. It is certainly not your intent to bore your listeners with the Word of God. On the contrary, you want to captivate minds and transform lives as you preach. But how? This book is part of the answer. I have spent the past twenty-one years as a pastor, church planter, and seminary professor committed to answering that question.

Years ago, as a young preacher trying to survive as the senior pastor in a church that expected a sermon from me three times a week, I only preached the New Testament letters. This was the literary genre I felt best prepared to preach. It was the biblical literature that my seminary professors had taught me to exegete and preach. With the benefit of many years of training I was able to preach a standard "three points and a poem" sermon with some effect.

As time went on, however, I realized that there were at least two reasons why I could not restrict my preaching to the epistles. First, it would not take long to run out of epistles to preach. You go through a lot of material when you are preaching three times a week! If I did not want to have to change churches every three years, I would have to widen the scope of my preaching. Second, I became convinced that if, like the apostle Paul, I was to "proclaim ... the whole will of God" (Acts 20:27), I simply had to learn to effectively communicate biblical genres other than epistles. I would not serve my congregation well if I fed them an interminable diet of Romans, Galatians, and 1 Corinthians. I realized that I was under divine obligation to preach all of Scripture, not just my favorite parts. Since narrative literature is the dominant genre of the Bible, it seemed like a good place to begin.

After announcing that I would begin a new sermon series from 1 Samuel on Sunday nights, I began studying in earnest. I survived the first few weeks of this fledgling series by essentially repreaching sermons I had heard growing up in the church. My problem came when I ran out of other people's material and had to do my own exegetical and homiletical work. It was then that I realized I did not know how to preach narrative literature. Why was Dagon falling to pieces every night? What was with these rats and tumors of gold? Who cared? How was I supposed to preach this stuff and who would want to listen if I did?

I faced a crisis in my study one week when I realized that I did not have the foggiest idea how to preach narrative literature. I could not continue my series. What could I do? I did what any respectable minister in my denomination would do. I arranged for missionaries to speak the next three Sunday nights, fled back to the safety of the epistles, and hoped that no one would notice that my new sermon series had been amputated.

Nobody ever asked me why we suddenly switched sermon series. Perhaps they never noticed. But I have never forgotten my agony in the study that week. That aborted sermon series served as a launching pad for my passion for preaching biblical narrative. I simply had to discover what the stories of Scripture meant and how to best communicate them. I could not plead helplessness when it came to the dominant literary form in all of Scripture. As a pastor, I knew that I *had* to learn how to preach biblical narratives — and to do so in a way that would grip the minds and transform the lives of my listeners.

In the pages that follow, you will discover what I have learned along the way. You will find out how to understand the stories of Scripture and how to communicate them with integrity. My goal is to help you learn how to preach the stories of Scripture in an irresistible, unforgettable, life-transforming fashion, and to do so without a hint of theological compromise.

Christ told Peter to "feed my sheep," but sleeping lambs do not eat. If we preachers cannot captivate people's minds, we will never capture their souls. A well-known Chinese curse says, "May you live in interesting times." When it comes to preaching the narrative literature of the Bible, this curse becomes my prayer. May your congregation live in interesting times as you preach the stories of Scripture.

Chapter One

WHY PREACH EXPOSITORY FIRST-PERSON SERMONS?

People in the pew don't need much time to develop a sense of what a "proper" sermon "should" look like. What people have seen from the pulpit in the past often shapes their expectations in the present. Many churches come equipped with self-appointed volunteers eager to inform pastors who happen to "preach outside the lines" of their ecclesiastical traditions. New pastors quickly discover what length, tone, and form of sermon address is expected by their new flock.

In light of this widespread resistance to homiletical change, why would any preacher with a mortgage want to introduce first-person sermons? If new sermon forms have the potential to cause pastoral unrest, why bother? Why not play it safe and be satisfied with preaching your father's sermon? Why not just rerun Martin Luther and Charles Spurgeon? Why preach first-person sermons? Why read the rest of this book? Because this homiletical form will enable your ministry in the pulpit to reach new levels of effectiveness. I am convinced that for cultural, educational, theological, and emotional reasons it is in your best interest to invest the time to read on — and discover how to preach effective first-person sermons.

> **A first-person** sermon communicates the idea of a biblical passage through a character with personal knowledge of the events in the passage. Preachers take on the personality of this character and reexperience the events of the biblical text in order to recommunicate what the original author communicated to the first recipients of the biblical narrative.

Cultural Reasons for First-Person Sermons

Plan on curling up with a good book tonight? If so, you are a rarity. People are increasingly choosing to reach for their remotes and spend their nights in the glow of a silver screen. We love our television sets, movie theaters, and DVDs.

When introduced in 1946, only a few thousand viewers bothered to watch television. In the 1951–1952 season, however, two new shows were introduced: *I Love Lucy* and *Dragnet*. The popularity of these shows was so overwhelming that the sales of TV sets skyrocketed. By 1954, over half of all the households in the nation were watching television.[1]

Almost fifty years later, the influence of television is stronger than ever.[2] By the time they reach eighteen, children have watched an average of seven years of television. According to the New York Academy of Medicine, "children spend more time in front of the television than in school, and nearly as much time as they spend sleeping." And children are not the only ones glued to the tube. Television viewing is now the #1 adult leisure activity in America. And what happens when "nothing's on"? We often catch a movie on the big screen or slip a DVD into our home theater system.

According to the Motion Picture Association of America, business is booming. Box office receipts in the U.S. increased from $7 billion in 1998 to $9.5 billion in 2002. In 2002 alone, movie attendance increased by 10 percent. While people enjoy going to see first-run movies, they don't seem to mind recycled movies either. The video rental business is booming.

Sixty-four percent of the U.S. population lives within a ten-minute drive of a Blockbuster store. Forty-eight million of those people have a Blockbuster account. Over three million people a day drop by their local Blockbuster for a movie. No wonder this company enjoyed worldwide revenues of $5.5 billion in 2002.

Why are we drawn to all of these screens? Why do we spend so much of our time under their influence? It's not because of the popcorn — it's because of the stories. Television sells stories. Look at the top-rated shows. Virtually all of them are narratives. Hollywood also hawks stories. Bigger screens just mean bigger budget stories. And Blockbuster makes its billions peddling its slightly used plots on the street corner. We live in a story-saturated society.

Narrative has triumphed, and all of this drama has left its mark on the American mind. "This extraordinary chunk of time Americans spend under the influence of narrative . . . has left its imprint."[3] It has changed the way people prefer to communicate. Today's gentlemen (and ladies) prefer stories — even when they go to church. Wise preachers recognize the preference of their parishioners and capitalize on it in their preaching. They don't restrict their preaching to Paul's letters.

Most of us learned to preach the New Testament epistles while we were in seminary, and only the epistles. Today we feel comfortable creating mechanical outlines from Romans 5, but we are unsure of what to do with other genres. It's time to grow. We need to learn how to preach the whole counsel of God. Our homiletical horizons have to expand until they include the narratives of Scripture.

The best way to communicate to a story-loving society is with stories. The best way to preach to this society is by utilizing the stories of Scripture. It's a good thing God uses so many of them. Narratives are the dominant genre in the Bible. In order to be faithful to the Word and effective to our culture, we need to learn to preach the stories of Scripture. First-person sermons are an excellent way to communicate narrative literature to our narrative society.

If you want to be heard and understood, you must speak in the way that people can best hear you. If the world switches from FM to satellite radio, so must we. It would be tragic to broadcast a critical message on a frequency that many people are no longer using. We squander opportunities for influence when we preach to bygone generations. We must communicate Scripture the way that people listen.

If we are to be as effective as Luther and Spurgeon were in their generations, we must be as contemporary as they were. To make maximum impact on our society we must communicate the Scripture the way that people can best hear and respond.

Educational Reasons for First-Person Sermons

One of the major goals of a biblical sermon should be instruction. And for good reason: The New Testament frequently relates biblical knowledge with spiritual maturity.

The apostle Paul told the Colossian Christians that the reason "we proclaim him, admonishing and teaching everyone with all wisdom, [is] so that we may present everyone perfect [or mature] in Christ" (Col. 1:28). It seems that understanding factual information about the person of Jesus Christ is essential for those who aspire to spiritual maturity.

Likewise, the writer of the book of Hebrews encourages his readers to "leave the elementary teachings about Christ and go on to maturity, not laying again the foundation of repentance from acts that lead to death, and of faith in God, instruction about baptisms, the laying on of hands, the resurrection of the dead, and eternal judgment" (Heb. 6:1–2). It seems that Christians who are content with an elementary understanding of Scripture are permanently stuck in a juvenile spiritual state.

Paul urges Timothy, a young aspiring preacher, not to forget "how from infancy you have known the holy Scriptures, which are able to make you wise for salvation through faith in Christ Jesus. All Scripture is God-breathed and is useful for teaching, rebuking, correcting and training in righteousness, so that the man of God may be thoroughly equipped for every good work" (2 Tim. 3:15–17). Like our first-century predecessor, we dare not forget how important our growth in Bible knowledge has been to our own spiritual development and how critical it is in the spiritual development of others.

Some preachers are understandably critical regarding first-person sermons. They ask:

- Will this type of sermon actually teach my congregation?
- It seems like entertainment! Is this another Neil Postman example[4] of contemporary society amusing itself to intellectual death?
- I know that people enjoy this type of sermon, but will they grow from it?
- Hosea said that "my people are destroyed from lack of knowledge. Because you have rejected knowledge, I also reject you as my priests; because you have ignored the law of your God, I also will ignore your children" (Hos. 4:6). Will I be guilty of injuring my flock by feeding them first-person sermons?

These legitimate questions and educational concerns are best addressed within the context of education theory. Almost all educational theorists understand that different individuals have different preferred learning styles. One of the most articulate spokespeople in this field is Howard Gardner.[5] He argues that there is not one type of intelligence. People process information in eight distinct ways.

- *Linguistic intelligence* — the capacity to use language to express what's on your mind and to understand other people (poets, orators, lawyers).
- *Logical-mathematical intelligence* — the ability to understand the underlying principles of some kind of a causal system, the way a scientist or a logician does; or to manipulate numbers, quantities, and operations, the way a mathematician does.
- *Spatial intelligence* — the ability to represent the spatial world in one's mind, the way a sailor or airplane pilot navigates the large spatial world, or the way a chess player or sculptor represent a more circumscribed spatial world. The spatially intelligent are often employed as painters, sculptors, and architects or in sciences such as anatomy or topology.
- *Bodily kinesthetic intelligence* — the aptitude to use one's body (or part of the body) to solve a problem, make something, or put on some kind of production. Examples include athletics and performing arts such as dance or acting.
- *Musical intelligence* — the endowment to think in music, to be able to hear patterns, recognize them, remember them, and manipulate them.
- *Interpersonal intelligence* — the ability to understand other people, as seen in teachers, clinicians, salespersons, and politicians. Those who deal with other people have to be skilled in the interpersonal sphere.

- *Intrapersonal intelligence* — having an understanding of yourself, knowing who you are, what you can do, what you want to do, how you react to things, which things to avoid, and which things to gravitate toward.
- *Naturalist intelligence* — the human ability to discriminate among living things (plants, animals) as well as sensitivity to other features of the natural world (e.g., clouds, rock configurations). It is an essential intelligence for the botanist and chef.[6]

In the same way that all people are somewhat visually unique, so people are also cognitively distinct. We think in unique ways.

> What makes life interesting . . . is that we don't have the same strength in each intelligence area, and we don't have the same amalgam of intelligences. Just as we look different from one another and have different kinds of personalities, we also have different kinds of minds.[7]

The educational implications of these cognitive differences are staggering. It means that both in the classroom and in the pulpit, there is no "ideal"or "best" way for all people to learn. Thus, an ineffective preacher or teacher is one who uses a teaching method that is unduly reliant on one type of intelligence or learning preference. Those preachers who want the largest number of people to learn from their sermons should utilize what Gardner refers to as "multiple entry points."[8] They should use methods of teaching that harness as many intelligences or learning preferences as possible. The more entry points a sermon form touches on, the greater the number of people who will learn, and learn more effectively.

Some of the most effective multiple entry point sermon forms are narrative in shape. Consider, for example, how many intelligences can be stimulated through a single first-person narrative sermon. In such a message, the preacher is free to dramatically express linguistic intelligence. A first-person narrative sermon can be constructed in a way that is logical or that has the character to wrestle with underlying systems of thought. Some obvious advantages of first-person narrative messages are the way in which the spatial and bodily kinesthetic intelligences of the congregation are enlivened. A display of musical intelligence is not normally, but could easily be, integrated into a first-person narrative message. Likewise, a first-person narrative message could be readily scripted to touch the mind of the interpersonally and intrapersonally gifted individuals. The setting and scenery of any first-person narrative message (or the utilization of a naturalistic metaphor) could also create special interest in the mind of the naturalistically inclined church member.

While first-person sermons may be entertaining, they are not the educational equivalent of candy floss or soda pop. They are nutritionally significant — often more educationally effective than more traditional sermon forms. In my experience, almost everyone loves a first-person sermon, and almost everyone learns from them.

First-person sermons enable preachers to communicate biblical truth to a wide spectrum of people and learning preferences. When preachers stand Sunday mornings and preach a first-person sermon, they are not necessarily substituting glitz for content. On the contrary, their multiple entry point capacity gives them educational credibility. And responsible preachers can use them with confidence.

Theological Reasons for First-Person Sermons

Some preachers object to first-person sermons on theological grounds. To be legitimate, they argue, a sermon must have points (preferably three) that (ideally) begin with the same letter. While they may concede that there is some cultural and educational validity of this "radical" sermon form, they would also argue that there is no biblical or theological necessity to preach first-person sermons or to utilize any type of narrative homiletical structure. I disagree. I think a conservative evangelical approach to Scripture demands that preachers utilize narrative homiletical forms, including first-person sermons. Here's why.

The Inspiration of Scripture

> God inspired human writers to choose the precise language symbols (words) he wanted to communicate his purposes.

I believe that the Bible is more than just inspiring literature. It is also divinely inspired literature.

The Bible was written by individuals whose wills were so commingled with that of the Holy Spirit that the words they wrote were equally their own and God's. The Bible has been verbally inspired; under the influence of the Holy Spirit, human writers chose the precise words God wanted to communicate his purposes. As a result, the Bible contains the inerrant and infallible words of God.

> Above all, you must understand that no prophecy of Scripture came about by the prophet's own interpretation. For prophecy never had its origin in the will of man, but men spoke from God as they were carried along by the Holy Spirit. (2 Peter 1:20–21)

God's work of inspiration influenced more than just the word choices of the biblical writers. I believe that God's work of inspiration extended even to the arrangement of those words. Both the words and genre of the biblical text were inspired by the Holy Spirit.

Why must a high view of inspiration expand to include genre? Because in the communication process, the choice of genre significantly influences meaning. Let me illustrate. On the day of our twentieth wedding anniversary my wife, Nola, and I were apart. I was speaking at an international convention of the Gideon's in Charlotte, North Carolina, while Nola patiently waited for me to join her for a long-planned getaway to Miami Beach. While I may not be the most sensitive husband, I was aware that I needed to communicate to her on the day of our anniversary. I also knew what I wanted to say. I wanted to tell her that:

> God inspired human writers to choose the precise literary genres (arrangement of words) through which he wanted to communicate his purposes.

- for twenty years she has been God's greatest blessing in my life.
- her wisdom and support had helped me achieve whatever success in life and ministry I had experienced.
- I could hardly wait to spend another twenty years of life and ministry with her.
- I loved her more today than ever before.

These were the words I wanted to say, but how should I communicate them? What genre should I use? Certainly I had options.

What if I had decided to communicate that message in mathematical code? Certainly that would have been possible. According to Tom Clancy spies do it all the time! Do you think that my purposes would have been helped by using this genre? No? What if I had decided to communicate these words in the form of a limerick? Would that literary genre have helped or hindered my communicating a message of love? Or what if I had used the genre of an obituary? Would my wife have felt loved in Miami if I had chosen to express my feelings in the way we generally honor the deceased? Probably not. The problem with mathematical codes, limericks, and obituaries is not that they are not legitimate means of communication. They are. But good communicators understand the importance of matching messages with appropriate genres.

The correct genre can enhance and support a message; the wrong genre can distort and even destroy a message. Communication theorist Marshall McLuhan was right when he said that in the communication process, "environments are not passive wrappings, but are, rather, active processes which are invisible."[9] Genre is not neutral. It actively influences meaning just as surely as the selection of words. God and the human authors of Scripture understood this. Together they chose the most appropriate genre for the message they were communicating. As Ronald Allen said:

The form of the text — its particular configuration of words, images, thoughts — cannot be separated from the meaning of the text, because it is precisely through the form that the fullness of the text's meaning is imparted . . . the form itself is an embodiment of meaning.[10]

The Purpose of the Sermon

> God's inspired combination of word and genre is adequate to communicate his ideas.

A primary goal of a preacher is to communicate and apply the primary idea intended by the original author of a unit of Scripture. Good preaching is not based on an original idea. It strives to say to a contemporary audience what the original author of the biblical text said to the original audience. It is to say what God said.

There is a sense in which a biblical sermon is like a cell phone call. In a biblical text, God is placing a call. He has a message he wants to communicate to his church. In order for the cell phone call to make it to its intended recipients, however, it must be successfully passed through a series of repeater stations. Preachers are like cell phone repeater stations. Our purpose is to pass on God's message to its intended recipients without altering the message in any way. We are only successful when God's voice is passed on to God's people without any distortion of any kind.

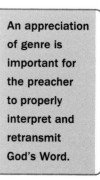

> An appreciation of genre is important for the preacher to properly interpret and retransmit God's Word.

"The sermon's task is to extend a portion of the text's impact into a new communicational situation. . . . Since the text achieves its rhetorical impact through its particular literary form . . . the preacher's task . . . [is] . . . to regenerate the impact . . . of . . . the text."[11] The only way that we can communicate God's Word with this kind of clarity is by taking note of genre. Genre has to influence our homiletics as much as our exegesis. It is impossible for a preacher to reproduce the meaning of the text without making homiletical allowance for the original genre of the text.

> [Because of] . . . the close relationship between form and content . . . one cannot simply take the content of a biblical form, like milk in a container, and pour it indiscriminately into a different form. In literature, form and content are so intimately related that preachers must carefully select the appropriate form for the sermon if they would not distort the message of the text.[12]

The original author's intended message is most faithfully retransmitted if the form of the original message is acknowledged and preserved.

I do not preach first-person sermons in an effort to be cute or trendy. Nor am I overwhelmed by a desire to be relevant to our narrative-saturated culture. The primary reason I preach narrative passages of Scripture in a narrative style is to be faithful to the biblical text. I want to say what God said in the biblical text, and only what God said in the biblical text. I cannot be faithful to the meaning of the original text without being homiletically respectful of its genre.

The best way to preach the Bible's narrative literature is by using a narrative homiletical form. First-person sermons are a legitimate narrative homiletical form. When you learn how to preach this type of sermon, you learn how to preach the stories of Scripture with great accuracy. You will also discover that just about everybody enjoys listening to them and that in the midst of their good time, your congregation is learning a tremendous amount of Bible.

Emotional Reasons for First-Person Sermons

But first-person sermons do even more. Although not a friend of the church, Charles Templeton spoke truthfully when he made the following observation about today's pulpit:

> It is incredible that so much contemporary preaching is boring. That the Christian message should bore anyone is itself astonishing. The Old Testament is replete with high drama and tenanted by wonderfully colourful characters. . . . Yet, somehow, many if not most preachers manage to transform the transforming message . . . into the pallid, innocuous moralism that proceeds from so many pulpits today.[13]

Why are so many sermons that originate from narrative literature so boring? The problem is not with the text. The great stories of Scripture are brimming with emotion and vitality. And when they were told in ancient Israel, I am sure that those who listened were deeply moved.

Consider the David and Goliath narrative as an example. When the story of David's triumph was originally told, it would have been done orally. An elder skilled in the art of oral tradition would have, in response to the requests of the community, gathered everyone around a fire at the end of the day. There, with the stars overhead and the business of the day long past, the village would hear of a heathen Philistine giant named Goliath. Goliath was a massive brute who strutted in front of the armies of Israel for forty days and challenged them to a fight. For over a month this uncircumcised beast defied the king of Israel and the armies of Israel — and the God of Israel. Everyone cowered in front of him. Nobody was willing to take on Goliath. The battle seemed as if it was over before it began. Until a ruddy little boy from the back side of nowhere wandered onto the scene.

David arrived on the battlefield on a grocery run for his father. He was young and unimpressive looking. His own father overlooked him. He had no military training or experience. Yet when he heard Goliath's rants, he instantly responded. David was so convinced of the faithfulness of his God that he volunteered to do what no one else in the nation would do: fight Goliath. It looked as if David didn't have a chance. It was ridiculous to see David walking down the hill towards Goliath armed only with a stick and a sling. Even Goliath roared his disapproval.

How do you think the people of the village would have responded a few moments later when, with their imaginations, they heard David's smooth stone whistling through the wind? And when they witnessed Goliath's eyes open wide in dull surprise. And then they observed David using Goliath's sword to remove his head. How do you think the villagers would have responded?

I think that the mothers would have covered the ears of their little ones during the description of the gory bits. And I think the kids would have tried to pry

The Preaching Task at a Glance

Pressing your nose against a television screen will not give you a better understanding of your favorite television show. The pixels that flicker on your television screen are meaningless when viewed individually. Their significance only becomes apparent when you back away from the screen. A broader perspective is necessary to appreciate those pixels. Details need distance. This is also true of the preaching process.

Let's get a "bird's-eye" view of the preaching task before we focus on the details, or "worm's-eye" view, of sermon preparation. This will help the details fall into place. We need distance to gain perspective.

- Preaching can be very complicated. It can also be very simple.
- Every sermon has a beginning. It starts when you receive your preaching assignment. At that moment, the preaching process has begun.

Every sermon also has an end. There is a time when it is all over. The preaching task ends when the last song has been sung, the benediction has been delivered,

and you are walking to the back of the church. For better or worse, for richer or poorer, the sermon is now over and done.

(Beginning) |———————————→| (End)

Truly biblical sermons, however, have something else. They also have middle point. If the goal of the preacher is to communicate the idea that the biblical writer originally communicated, then the preacher must divide the sermon preparation task into two disparate stages: the exegetical and the homiletical. The diagram below may be more appropriate.

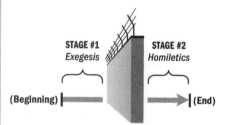

STAGE #1
Exegesis

STAGE #2
Homiletics

(Beginning) |——————   ——→| (End)

Stage 1: The first task of the preacher is exegetical: determining the *meaning* of the text. Your goal here is to discover the idea that the original author intended to communicate to the original audience. In this stage, you are like a miner, using your exegetical skills to dig deeply into their Mom's hands away so that they could hear the gory bits. I think that the young boys and girls would run off into the darkness, sending stones flying off into the darkness pretending they were David. I think that the young men would be standing silently in the darkness, wondering if they would be willing to demonstrate the faith and courage of David. I think that some of the old men would have had a tear running down their cheek, as they remembered back to what it was like to have a true man of God lead his people.

But when preachers today proclaim the same text under the title "The Five Secrets of the Happy Christian Life," people today are not moved to tears — only to sleep. Why do so many of today's sermons fail to communicate the stories of

the biblical text to unearth the treasure it contains. This is our sole obsession.

Stage 2: The second task of the preacher is homiletical: determining the best way to *communicate* the idea of the text. It is not enough for the biblical idea to be clear in your mind. You need to develop a strategy for transferring that idea to the minds of your audience. The challenge here is to create a setting for this newly discovered exegetical jewel that will best display its unique attributes.

It is critical that you keep these two stages distinct. *Do not blend the two stages together.* If you begin to think homiletically too soon (how will I preach this?) during your exegesis, you will inadvertently pollute the exegetical process. Thinking about outlines, introductions, and possible applications prematurely will prevent the biblical text from speaking for itself. When the two stages begin to bleed together, it is easy to miss the author's idea. What you end up preaching may be theologically correct but not what the original author intended to communicate to the original audience. If your goal is only to say what God said, then I recommend you imagine these two stages separated by a wall: tall, thick, and impenetrable — with razor wire on

top. This wall separates the two separate stages of the sermon preparation process. It cannot be scaled. It cannot be breached.

One way of keeping these tasks discrete is by playing a simple mind game. I pretend that I am still a seminary student and that my professor has just given me an exegetical assignment. According to the syllabus of this make-believe class, all that is required is an accurate exegetical analysis of the passage. I will never have to preach this text. Sunday will never arrive. My interest in this passage is purely intellectual.

The purity of this intellectual pursuit helps me from using the text for my own well-intentioned purposes. It encourages me to surrender to the agenda of the original writer and to overhear what the ancient author said to the ancient audience. It helps me to exegete with integrity.

Only after the exegesis is completed can I move onto the second phase of the preaching task. That impenetrable wall does have a door. The only way to open it and to pass from stage 1 to stage 2 is by using the proper key — a key shaped in the form of the "big idea." Chapter 2 will help you find this key.

Scripture with ancient power? Because they don't use a homiletical form that is appropriate to the genre of the text.

For many preachers, unfortunately, seminary training in preaching merely furnished them with a set of homiletical cookie cutters, which they routinely mash down on the dough of the text, and presto! Out pops a little star, or a tree, or a gingerbread man. (A five pointed sermon? An organic sermon? A life-situation sermon?). No matter that the text doesn't want to go into these forms; the poor thing is mashed and tortured until it is made to say things it never intended to say.[14]

Benton Lutz was correct in his observation that "pastors (often) force stale, dry words into our heads rather than telling the stories in ways that illuminate our lives. They do not crack the kerygma open and let those stories spill over into the events of our daily lives."[15] As Fred Craddock has pointed out:

> If the minister wants the sermon to do what the text does, then he or she will want to hold on to the form, since form captures and conveys function, not only during the interpretation of the text but during the designing of the sermon as well. . . . One does not want to move too far from the form of the text. Much preaching that aims at propositions and themes and outlines does just that: the minister boils off all the water and then preaches the stain in the bottom of the cup.[16]

Expository first-person sermons help preachers increase the impact of their messages. They are the most effective way to communicate both the emotion and the truth of a narrative passage. These sermons capture the mind and inflame the imagination. They persuade listeners that the Bible is alive and relevant. Preachers who choose to communicate narrative literature with a first-person sermon are choosing to release the natural emotion of those texts. They are choosing to preach dynamic, exciting messages.

©2002 Tribune Media Services, Inc. All Rights Reserved. Reprinted with permission.

NOTES FOR CHAPTER ONE

1. Joyce Nelson, *The Perfect Machine* (Toronto: Between the Lines, 1987), 46.
2. As quoted by Shelley Thorpe in *www.idahochild.org* (accessed Sept. 23, 2003).
3. Timothy A. Turner, *Preaching to a Programmed People* (Grand Rapids: Kregel, 1995), 20.

4. Neil Postman, *Amusing Ourselves to Death* (New York: Penguin, 1986).

5. Howard Gardner is a professor in the Graduate School of Education at Harvard University and a researcher at the Veterans Administration Medical Center in Boston. A foundational book is his *Frames of Mind: The Theory of Multiple Intelligences* (New York: Basic Books, 1983).

6. Adapted from Kathy Checkley, "The First Seven . . . and the Eighth," *Educational Leadership* (September 1997), 12.

7. Howard Gardner, in the interview by Kathy Checkley, "The First Seven . . . and the Eighth," *Educational Leadership* (September 1997), 9.

8. "My research has suggested that any rich, nourishing topic . . . can be approached in . . . ways that, roughly speaking map on to the multiple intelligences. We might think of the topic as a room with . . . (various) doors or entry points into it. Students vary as to which entry point is most appropriate for them. Awareness of these entry points can help the teacher introduce new materials in ways in which they can be easily grasped by a range of students" (Howard Gardner, *Multiple Intelligences: The Theory in Practice* [New York: Basic Books, 1993], 203).

9. Marshall McLuhan and Quentin Fiore, *The Medium Is the Message* (SanFranciso: Hardwired, 1967), 68.

10. Ronald J. Allen, "The Language of the Text," in Don M. Wardlaw, *Preaching Biblically* (Philadelphia: Westminster, 1983), 32.

11. Thomas G. Long, *Preaching and the Literary Forms of the Bible* (Philadelphia: Fortress, 1989), 33.

12. Sidney Greidanus, *The Modern Preacher and the Ancient Text* (Grand Rapids: Eerdmans, 1988), 147.

13. Charles Templeton, *Farewell to God* (Toronto: McClelland and Stewart, 1996), 159.

14. Clyde Fant, *Preaching for Today* (New York: Harper & Row, 1975), 110.

15. H. Benton Lutz, "The Self-Absorbed Masquerade," *The Other Side* 29/4 (July–August 1993): 46.

16. Fred B. Craddock, *Preaching* (Nashville: Abingdon, 1985), 123.

PART ONE

STEPS IN THE EXEGETICAL TASK

Chapter Two

BEGINNING TO USE THE NARRATIVE EXEGETICAL KEY: STEPS 1 AND 2

The stories of Scripture surprise us. We come to them with the assumption that they will be easy to understand. After all, how hard can a story be? Our grandparents read stories to us. We read them to our kids. But when we try to preach from 1 and 2 Samuel or the gospel of Luke, we can spend a frustrating number of hours at our desk trying to make sense out them. We discover that peering down the corridor of time into the mind of an ancient author is never easy and that narrative literature may be particularly difficult.

Kids may love stories, but they are definitely not child's play. They are a highly sophisticated art form that God has used as a communication vehicle. They can seem at times more like a Solomonic riddle than the plain revelation of God. In my moments of exegetical angst I have sometimes wished I had a magic formula to give me instant insight into these biblical texts. There isn't any. Incantations will not open the stories of Scripture to you. To discover the idea that the biblical author wrapped in a story of Scripture you must adopt a distinctively narrative exegetical approach.

It may surprise you to learn that there is no "one method fits all" exegetical methodology. Many of us came out of seminary with an assumption that what works for the epistles will work anywhere. It won't. Here you will need to use a new exegetical key — a key cut in the shape of a narrative. With this key, the door of understanding to huge portions of the Bible will begin to swing wide. Narratives will begin to make sense to you. It will become relevant to you — and preachable.

I encourage you to read through the eight steps beginning in this chapter and the following ones and give them a try. You know that *abracadabra* doesn't work.

Calvin and Hobbes ©1986 Watterson. Reprinted with permission of Universal Press Syndicate. All rights reserved.

STEP ONE | Adjust your interpretive paradigm.

More than History

Do you believe that the Bible is historically accurate? Are you convinced that when the Scriptures talk about historical events that those events actually occurred? That Jonah was a real man swallowed by a genuine fish? That Jesus trod on Jewish soil? And on top of the Sea of Galilee? I do. But does that mean that the Bible is a history book? No. The Bible contains history, but it is not a history book. The goal of the biblical writers is not to provide you with a comprehensive overview of world history.

I remember when this concept became very clear to me. I was looking after my two boys one Monday and decided to take them to the museum of natural history. When they walked into the building, their jaws dropped. They were in awe. They loved looking at the lions, tigers, and snow leopards that were on display. But what really got them excited were the dinosaur bones! Those mammoth skeletons stretched two stories above them. They were both intimidating and impressive. Then my oldest son turned to me and asked: "Dad, how come the Bible doesn't talk about dinosaurs?"

I was tempted for a moment to point out that there were oblique references to a leviathan in the book of Job. Then I realized that to do so would be avoiding the issue behind my son's question. What he really wanted to know was why such impressive-looking creatures had not been given top billing in the Bible. Why are no dinosaurs mentioned in the early chapters of Genesis? Did the biblical writers fail to do their homework? Were they unaware of these creatures? Of course not.

The reason that the Bible does not talk about dinosaurs (or a thousand other subjects that secular historians would have included in their books) is that the biblical writers did not need these items to accomplish their purpose. It was superfluous information. The goal of the biblical writers was not to give us an *Encyclopaedia Britannica* style overview of world events. The biblical narrators combed through the massive amounts of history available to them and selected only those events that served their unique purpose. What was their purpose? The communication of theological ideas.

Get to the Point

The writers of historical narrative did not intend to provide their readers with a comprehensive overview of world events. They were not interested in providing us with a well-rounded liberal arts education. They knew we could get that elsewhere. Instead, these writers, under the influence of the Holy Spirit, *used* history to communicate their *theological ideas*. Their goal was not simply to increase the general knowledge or broaden the cultural awareness of their audience. Biblical narrators wanted to tell us about God and about how humanity should live in response to who he is. They focused on ideas for good reason.

Ideas are the most powerful force in the world. They change the destiny of nations and individual lives. All of us live in response to the ideas that we hold. Do you believe in Darwin's idea of evolution? If so, that idea will have a profound influence on your life. Do you believe that Jesus is God and the only hope for a sin-infected humanity? If you do, that idea will change your life. We are controlled by our ideas.

Mother was wrong when she said, "You are what you eat." She should have said, "You are what you think." Change your ideas and you will change your life. Noble ideas result in noble lives. God's ideas will make your life resemble a tree planted by a river. This is why the apostle Paul said that we are to be "transformed by the renewing of [our] mind" (Rom. 12:2). We are what we believe. This is why the biblical writers were not satisfied with just giving historical content. They used history as a vehicle for their ideas.

The "historical books" of the Bible are not merely history books. They are theological works of art that display God to us and show how to live in response. Understanding that the Bible *uses history to communicate theological ideas* is critical for effective preaching. It pushes you beyond "what does the text say?" It forces you to ask, "What did the author mean?" It makes the preacher go beyond the facts of a story to the idea of the story. It makes the preacher aim higher, beyond content to intent.

Because most preachers enjoy history, there is a temptation to simply rehearse the "fascinating" details of the narratives when we preach the stories of Scripture. Contemporary scholarship has often encouraged this practice. If you survey nineteenth- and twentieth-century commentaries, you will find that a great deal of ink has flowed on subjects such as syntax, grammar, etymology, geography, historical chronology, and cultural backgrounds. This mass of information has frequently resulted in the suffocation of the primary idea of the text beneath a deluge of detail, much like a fog "which at first renders objects indistinct and then finally blots them out altogether."[1] We preachers must resist the temptation to say everything we know about a narrative passage and instead assert with crystal clarity the main idea that all the details of the text are pointing to.

Your exegetical goal must be "to recover as accurately as possible the meaning that the original writer intended."[2] It is impossible to overstate the importance of adopting this agenda. You cannot begin to prepare a clear sermon until you are clear in your own mind what your text means.

The goal of this section is to enable you to write this kind of sentence.[3] Although writing this one sentence may be difficult, it is certainly the most important exegetical task. Without this sentence your first-person sermon may not say anything. Or worse, you may end up preaching something other than God intended. Getting the correct "big idea" will transform your message from tedious to tremendous and will allow the power of God's Word to transform the lives of your listeners. Keep your eye on the prize. Your goal is authorial intent, not just content! Don't settle for factoids. Communicate the big idea!

Appreciate the Literature

One of the harmful side effects of much of liberal scholarship during the past century has been its tendency to denigrate the literary quality of biblical narrative. This scholarship encouraged us to view the stories of Scripture as the work of a number of rather clumsy editors (who in Old Testament studies were often referred to as JEDP). We were told that these editors tried to refashion the stories to accomplish their own agendas. The result was less than perfect, often confusing and frequently a self-contradicting piece of literature. I disagree.

The stories of Scripture are not examples of bad writing. The careful literary analysis that has gone on during the past few decades has shown them to be masterful works of art. When theological agendas are laid aside, we are able to appreciate the narratives for what they really are: literature extraordinaire. In 1984, Leland Ryken wrote, "There is a quiet revolution going on in the study of the Bible. At its center is a growing awareness that the Bible is a work of literature and that the methods of literary scholarship are a necessary part of any complete study of the Bible."[4] The literary revolution has not stopped.

There is a growing recognition that C. S. Lewis was correct when he said that "the Bible, since it is literature, cannot be properly read except as literature; and the different parts of it as the different sorts of literature they are. . . . Otherwise we shall miss what is in them and think we see what is not."[5] And what fine literature it is. As Hermann Gunkel has pointed out, "even . . . the oldest legends of Genesis [are not] aimless, rude stories, tossed off without reflection, but on the contrary, there is revealed in them a mature, perfected, and very forcible art."[6]

Even the respected literary critic Northrop Frye, who personally rejected the truth claims of Scripture, could not help but acknowledge its literary nature. For many years he taught a course in biblical literature at the University of

Toronto because "I soon realized that a student of English literature who does not know the Bible does not understand a good deal of what he reads. . . . I offered a course in the English Bible as a guide to the study of English literature."[7] Not only is the Bible literature, but it also is one of the most influential literary works ever written. Frye sympathetically quotes and adopts William Blake's description of the Bible as the "Great Code of Art."

The Bible is not just a religious book. It is the most influential work of literature ever written. The Bible is the gold standard of literature. All other literature stands in its shadow. E. J. Young was correct when he entitled his book *Thy Word Is Truth*, for the Bible is truth. But it is more than truth. It is also ripping good literature. And all who want to exegete it must remember and respect its literary attributes.

The extraordinary literary quality of the biblical narratives should not surprise us, at least not if we take the doctrine of inspiration seriously. If Scripture really is "God-breathed" as it claims to be, you would expect it to radiate only the finest of literary qualities. And it does. From beginning to end, the Scriptures display the beauty of the creator God.

The God of the Bible loves beauty. If you doubt this, take a moment and look around at what he made. Look at the bride walking down that aisle. Gaze at the tiny perfection of a newborn baby. Look up at the heavens in the dead of the night. Look out the window of your car; whether you are driving in New England or New Mexico, the beauty is breathtaking. God made it all. He loves beauty and creativity. And it only makes sense that his creative fingerprints are seen on the book he inspired.

The God who loves beauty has inspired beautiful literature. Thus, those who want to understand God's literature must take the time to appreciate its subtle and complex beauty. Interpreters must recognize the inherent literary qualities of this literature. The significance of the literary nature of Scripture on the interpretive process should not be minimized. As Leland Ryken points out:

> Literature has its own forms and techniques. Before we can understand what a piece of literature says, we need to scrutinize the form in which it says it. . . . The literary critic's preoccupation with the how of biblical writing is not frivolous. It is a quest for understanding as well as enjoyment. In a literary text, it is impossible to separate what is said from how it is said, content from form.[8]

These stories rank among the finest literature ever written. They are not poorly stitched together myths. Every detail is intentional and significant. They are actual events cradled in a literary vehicle that was carefully created to accomplish a specific spiritual agenda. They are literary history and must be interpreted as such. The steps that follow in this chapter are designed to help you find the main idea of the stories of Scripture while appreciating its literary characteristics.

Understand the larger context of the story you want to preach.

Many of us are guilty of regularly taking a "quick and dirty approach" to sermon preparation, and we know why. Life is busier than ever in the pastorate. Our watches go too fast. We simply cannot find the time we need to tick off all the items on the "to do" list on our PDAs. And so we succumb to the tempting voice of expediency and immediately zero in on the specific verses we want to preach, without taking the time to examine the book that plays host for those words. We pull out our exegetical electron microscopes before we look at a map.

To do this is to commit an almost unrecoverable exegetical error. You must know what continent you are on before you launch into a subatomic investigation of its flora and fauna. You cannot understand your text unless you understand its context. As Old Testament scholar (and former faculty colleague of mine) Douglas Stewart says so often: "Context is king!" To faithfully communicate a biblical narrative you must understand the book from which it comes. Take the time to ask: "What is the larger context of your story?"

When Was the Book Written?

Biblical communication does not take place in a vacuum. It is reactive. God is responding to a preexisting situation. To understand *why* a book was written you first need to know *when* it was written. In narrative interpretation, timing is everything.

Don't panic at the mention of dates. It is probably not necessary to determine the exact year a book was written. What you do want to understand, however, is where the narrative fits within the overall flow of biblical history.

When you know who the author of a narrative was, the matter of dating is fairly straightforward. You already know that the gospels were written by the men whose names they bear, and that Luke also wrote the book of Acts. Because we know this, we also know that their books were written within a few decades of the death of Christ. The issue of dating the New Testament narratives is fairly straightforward. When you turn to the Old Testament, however, the issue of dating becomes much more difficult.

If you accept Mosaic authorship of the Pentateuch, determining the *approximate* time it was written is possible. Let's do it together. When do you think Moses would have written his five books?

- Is it likely that Moses wrote them when he was a young prince of Egypt? Perhaps as his doctoral dissertation? If not, why not? I do not think that he had the spiritual maturity at this point in his life to write the spiritually significant material we find here. And besides, most of the events mentioned in these books had not yet occurred. The Pentateuch could not have been written so early.

- Is it likely that Moses did his writing immediately after his burning bush experience? No, for the same reasons just mentioned.
- How about after he had led the people of God out of Egypt and delivered the law to them at Sinai? Do you think that Moses immediately sat down and wrote the Pentateuch then? Not very likely. In addition to the reasons mentioned previously, there is also the matter of time. The narrative does not leave room for the time necessary to write a book the length and quality of the first five books of the Bible. If you have ever tried writing a book, you know that it does not happen in a weekend!
- Immediately after leaving Sinai, Moses led Israel to the very edge of the Promised Land and sent in twelve spies to scout out the territory. Two of them returned saying, "Go for it," but the other ten objected: "We can't attack those people; they are stronger than we are.... We seemed like grasshoppers" (Num. 13:31, 33). In other words, if we cross the Jordan River, we will be squashed like bugs! And they didn't cross the river. Moses did not have time to write Scripture while all this was going on.
- What happened next? The people of Israel spent the next forty years in the desert taking a route that looks in desperate need of a good GPS. Did Moses have time to write his books now? Yes. This is the period of Moses' life when it is most likely that he wrote the Pentateuch. During this time he had the opportunity, maturity, and (as we will see later) motivation to write the Pentateuch. Knowing when Moses did his writing is an important interpretive clue to understanding the Pentateuch.

It may surprise you to learn, however, that outside of the Pentateuch, we do not know who wrote most of the rest of the narrative literature in the Old Testament. To determine the date they were written, we will have to rely on the internal evidence that they contain.

Look for the latest events mentioned in the book. While the book of Ruth feels timeless when you read it, the narrator tips his chronological hand when he ends the book by mentioning that Ruth's son, Obed, was an ancestor of the famous King David. For the original recipients to find any significance in this detail, the book was most likely written after David had become a significant individual.

Look for anachronisms within the narratives. These are distinctive descriptions of people, places, or events that reveal the times of the writer. An example of how anachronisms can be helpful in determining date can be found in

1 Chronicles 29:7: "They gave toward the work on the temple of God five thousand talents and ten thousand *darics* of gold, ten thousand talents of silver, eighteen thousand talents of bronze and a hundred thousand talents of iron" (italics added). The careful reader will note that *darics* did not exist in David's day. This must be the currency of the writer's own day. Knowing this can help you establish an approximate date for the story you want to preach.

Look for revealing comments by the narrator. Sometimes the narrator will insert an explanatory comment into a narrative. Narrators used these comments to give their contemporary audiences a fuller understanding of ancient stories. Their explanations serve as helpful hints for contemporary interpreters in determining the date of the narratives.

As an example of establishing timing on the basis of the narrator's comments we will look at Ruth 4:6–8:

> At this, the kinsman-redeemer said, "Then I cannot redeem it because I might endanger my own estate. You redeem it yourself. I cannot do it."
>
> (Now in earlier times in Israel, for the redemption and transfer of property to become final, one party took off his sandal and gave it to the other. This was the method of legalizing transactions in Israel.)
>
> So the kinsman-redeemer said to Boaz, "Buy it yourself." And he removed his sandal.

In verse 7 the narrator clearly indicates that this book was written significantly later than the events it mentions. By the time the book of Ruth was written, the practice of passing sandals to confirm legal transactions was no longer observed. It was ancient history.

Once you know approximately when the book you are going to preach from was written, you are ready to ask yourself: To whom was this book written? Who were the receivers of this act of communication?

Who Was the Target Audience of This Book?

It is easier to understand communication if you know the people involved. I discovered this truth by accident.

Many years ago, my mother asked me to go up into her bedroom and get some clothing out of her dresser drawer. This was not an everyday request. I rarely entered my parents' bedroom and never would have had the gall to rummage through a drawer filled with her "unmentionables" without her permission. But my mother was doing laundry in the basement and didn't want to climb all those stairs. As an obedient teenager, I obeyed my mother.

As I was retrieving her garments, however, my hand brushed up against something hard at the back of the drawer. It was an old book. A diary. I don't know what you would have done in that situation. I yielded to temptation. And

I couldn't believe what I was reading. The entries, dating back to my mother's high school days, were a first-person account of some of the boys she was sweet on! I could not put it down. As the pages turned, so did my mother's affection. It was not long before she began writing about a young man that she found particularly interesting—a young man named "Jack." This was my father! Guilt forced me to quickly close the tattered book and put it back where I found it. I can assure you, however, that knowing the people involved did not lessen my interest in this literature. On the contrary, it made reading it almost irresistible! It took every bit of willpower I could find to put the book down and rush the slightly delayed and soiled clothing downstairs to my waiting mother.

Identifying the target audience of the New Testament letters is straightforward. They were written to the people they mention. Paul wrote to the church in Rome. The people he greeted in Romans 16 heard their names as the letter was read to the congregation. Priscilla and Aquilla were a flesh-and-blood couple who appreciated the time Paul took to thank them for their service to the Gentile church. But what is true of epistles is not true of New Testament narratives.

The target audience of the New Testament narratives was not the people mentioned on its pages. These stories were not written for the benefit of the characters they contain. They were evangelistic tools; written for various groups of unbelievers. Matthew, for example, seems to be addressing Jewish unbelievers. Luke appears to be tailoring his message for a Gentile audience. Determining the target audience will prevent you from preaching a generic gospel. It will allow you to preach them with the distinctiveness they deserve and the relevance and freshness that your audience deserves.

Determining the target audience of the Old Testament narratives is far more difficult. Like the New Testament narratives, these stories were not addressed to the people they mention. The book of Exodus was not written to Moses. The book of Samuel was not written for Samuel. Or Saul. Or David. The book of Ruth was not written for Ruth. With the exception of Moses (who wrote the Pentateuch), none of these other heroes of the faith even read the books that bear their name. These books were penned at a much later date for the benefit of a later audience. The biblical narrator harnessed the history of these heroes in order to instruct a later generation of God's people, and it is critical that you recognize this in your exegesis. Taking the time to determine the original target audience of a narrative can transform your preaching.

Why Did the Original Author Write This Book?

When you know *when* the book was written and *to whom* the book was written, you can address the critical question of *purpose*. A book's purpose resides at the confluence of these questions. Purpose explains the author's motivation to write the narrative.

You have discovered the purpose of a book when the question the recipients are asking is being answered by the content of the book. It has a logical flow. It makes sense.

If the thrust of the book doesn't match the needs of the original audience, you have a problem. You need to go back and check your work. You are either misunderstanding the message of the book or the situation of the target audience. This is hard work. Is it worth it? You bet. When your understanding of date, target audience, and purpose converge, however, the result is magnificent. You are able to preach with a power, clarity, and relevance you could never have imagined possible.

Let me illustrate.

A number of years ago I decided to preach a series of messages from the book of Genesis. This seemed like a wonderful idea until I turned to the first chapter. Panic began to set in. Like many of you, I had heard many sermons preached from this text — all of them a polemic against Darwin. I felt that I was obligated, because of tradition and my conservative theology, to preach my own appendix to the Scopes trial, and to do so with rich references to science. One of my problems, however, was that I had not excelled in high school science, and it was a long time since I had been in high school.

My other problem was that I was ministering in a university town. My congregation was populated by professors who knew this field far better than I. Reading a few creation research magazines and throwing in some references to "carbon dating" and "radioactive isotopes" was simply not going to cut it. Did my lack of scientific training preclude me from preaching this chapter? Was I academically unqualified to preach this chapter? In the midst of my growing panic, I began to ask the questions:

- Who wrote this book?
- When was this book written?
- Who was the target audience of the book?
- What was the purpose of this book?
- How does this story contribute to the purpose of the entire book?

Who wrote the book? When was the book written?
As we discussed earlier, I believe that Moses wrote the book of Genesis during the last forty years of his life. He wrote it while a generation of Israelites who had been too fearful to cross the Jordan River wandered to their death.

Who was the target audience of the book?
Moses was writing for the emerging generation.

What was the purpose of the book?
He was writing what he thought was theologically necessary for them to survive and thrive in the land that God had promised to their ancestors. Moses was one of the most successful leaders of all time. What he accomplished as a

leader was amazing. But he did not have a perfect track record. He had failed to lead God's people across the muddy Jordan River and into their destiny. This was one of the most spectacular failures of Moses' life.

As the years slowly passed and Moses watched his faithless countrymen die in the desert, he decided to do with his pen what a subsequent sin prevented him from doing in person. He wrote a theology that Israel could use to survive and thrive as God's people in the Promised Land.

How does this story contribute to the purpose of the entire book?

I think Moses knew that all of his writing would be in vain, however, if Israel did not find the courage to succeed where they had previously failed. They needed to find the courage to cross the Jordan River. Moses had no reason to believe that inexperienced Joshua could succeed where he had failed. Joshua did not enjoy Moses' reputation as a proven leader. And I am sure that the older generation was careful to pass on tales about the giants who were inhabiting their Promised Land — tales that grew taller as the years passed. I have no doubt that Moses worried about how he could help this new generation find the faith that had eluded their fathers. I think that this is why Moses wrote Genesis 1.

The beautiful language of Genesis 1 demonstrates the care that Moses lavished on it. As he constructed this chapter, he deliberately placed great emphasis on the effortlessness with which God created the world and everything in it. He wanted Israel to know that God created everything that is, and did so without raising a sweat. Because the power of God's Word is limitless, Israel had nothing to fear. God could easily deal with any and every danger that might come their way. Since there was no challenge greater than their God, Israel could cross the river with confidence. Their all-powerful creator God was with them.

What I knew for sure was that Moses' purpose in writing Genesis 1 was not to refute Darwin. He couldn't have. Darwin had not been born yet. And while Genesis 1 is relevant to the important and ongoing discussion about evolution, my first responsibility as a preacher is to communicate the primary message that the original author communicated to his audience.

The following Sunday morning I preached what Moses intended to communicate to his original audience. I invited some creation research scientists to come and talk about the scientific implications of the text that evening. Understanding the larger context of your narrative allows you to communicate authorial intent.·

The biblical narratives stand with and apart from the stories of the secular world. Biblical narratives are theological literature divinely written by human authors to help God's people meet specific challenges of their day. When you understand this, you are well on your way to unlocking the meaning of the story you want to preach.

NOTES FOR CHAPTER TWO

1. A. Berkeley Mickelsen, *Interpreting the Bible* (Grand Rapids: Eerdmans, 1963), 37.
2. Donald R. Sunukjian, "The Homiletical Theory of Expository Preaching" (Ph.D. diss., Univ. of California, 1974), 167.
3. I am indebted to Haddon Robinson for introducing me to this concept. See Haddon Robinson, *Biblical Preaching*, 2nd ed. (Grand Rapids: Baker, 2001), 41.
4. Ibid., 11.
5. C. S. Lewis, *Reflections on the Psalms* (Glasgow: Collins, 1981 reprint ed.), 10.
6. Hermann Gunkel, *The Legends of Genesis* (New York: Schocken, 1964), 78.
7. Northrop Frye, *The Great Code: The Bible and Literature* (New York: Harcourt Brace, 1982), xii.
8. Leland Ryken, "Bible as Literature," in *Foundations for Biblical Interpretation*, ed. David S. Dockery, Kenneth A. Matthews, and Robert B. Sloan (Nashville: Broadman & Holman, 1994), 65.

Chapter Three

DETERMINING THE STORY'S STRUCTURE: STEP 3

Before we allow a physician to operate on a patient, we insist that he or she has a sophisticated understanding of human anatomy. The reason for this requirement is obvious. If you don't understand what is going on under the skin, you shouldn't cut it open. The results could be fatal. In the same way, it is not wise for a preacher to begin dissecting a passage of Scripture without a basic knowledge of how and why the literature works. To preach narratives without a basic knowledge of how and why they work is spiritually dangerous. It results in sermons that are deadly boring.

STEP THREE | **Determine the structure of your story.**

Scenes and Plot

Take note of the individual scenes. Scenes are the building blocks of narrative literature. They are the "chunks" of activity that make up a story. All stories, regardless of size, are made up of a sequence of individual scenes — the longer the story the greater the number of scenes. As Adele Berlin has pointed out so helpfully, the scenes of biblical narratives are like the frames from which films are made. Each one exists separately, and they are combined in a certain order to make the greater narrative, but an individual frame has no life of its own outside of the film as a whole.[1]

Scenes have no significance individually. It is only after they are joined together with other scenes to create a story that their individual contribution can be appreciated. Scenes are meaningless when viewed in isolation. Like bolts scattered on the garage floor, their value can only be appreciated when they have been attached to a larger and more sophisticated creation. It is only after the narrator has intelligently joined the individual scenes together to form a story that the small but critical contribution made by each scene can be appreciated.

Who determines which scenes are used and in what order? This is the primary job of the narrator who creates organizational structures that give stories coherence. Narrators impose order on disorder, meaning out of chaos. This narrative structure is called *plot*.

Through the development of plot, the narrator transforms apparently random events into a meaningful order. The literary skill of a particularly good narrator is demonstrated when the scenes are arranged so artfully that the plot gradually emerges in the consciousness of the reader. Good narrators, therefore, only include scenes that advance the plot since good literature does not have superfluous scenes. Since the Bible is good literature, the goal of the narrative exegete is to determine how each scene contributes to the larger story. You should be constantly asking:

- Why did the narrator include this scene?
- How does this scene advance the plot?
- How would the story be harmed if it were missing?

One thing is sure. If it appears to you that the story would have been better off without a particular scene, you do not correctly understand the plot. Biblical narrative is first-rate literature. The stories it contains are inspired. The joint products of humanity and deity, these stories are the best of the best. They contain no wasted words or superfluous scenes. Your task as interpreter is not only to identify the individual scenes, but also to understand how each scene contributes to the overall development of the story. When you understand how each scene contributes to the plot, you will be able to determine when a biblical story begins and ends.

Where does the story begin and end? You cannot understand (or preach) a story of Scripture if you do not know where it begins and ends. Determining these points is easier with shorter books such as Jonah or Esther and far more difficult with epic literature such as Genesis. Regardless of the level of difficulty, however, you must identify where your story begins and ends. How do you do this?

To determine where a story begins and ends, employ the following strategy. First, identify the conflict of the story you would like to preach. Conflict is the foundation of story — the most critical component. Just as plots are built on the bedrock of conflict, all narrative literature is organized around some kind of conflict. The conflict may be internal or external (it can take a myriad of different forms), but it must be present. No conflict — no story, no matter who the author is. I learned this from my mother.

I remember as a child how upset my mother was when she heard about a "so-called Christian author" who was writing stories for children — that featured a witch! How could a Christian author do such a thing? The author she was referring to was, of course, C. S. Lewis. And C. S. Lewis was very much a Christian. He was also a professor of literature. As a literary expert, Lewis knew that a story featuring a character like Aslan (good, gracious, and powerful) required a character like the witch (evil, selfish, and only slightly less powerful). If Aslan did not have an enemy, Lewis would not have had a story.

Conflict is to story what wet is to water. You cannot have one without the other. When the conflict is resolved, the story is over. Ask yourself:

- What is the conflict in this story?
- What is the problem/source of tension that the main character of your narrative is facing?

Second, note how the narrator has strategically arranged the scenes of the story to gradually increase the intensity of the conflict experienced by the characters and, simultaneously, the amount of emotional tension experienced by the reader. Trace the increasing tension as it builds from scene to scene until it reaches an unbearable level. It is at this point of greatest tension when suddenly (and often surprisingly) the tension of the story is resolved — almost always with a happy ending. Stories begin with conflict and the emotional tension this creates, and end when the conflict and tension end. The key to understanding where biblical stories begin and end lies in appreciating the role conflict plays in narrative literature.

The Mono-Mythic Cycle

You can gain an even more sophisticated understanding of your story's use of conflict by using the Mono-Mythic Cycle.[2] This simple diagram allows you to visualize how storytellers harness conflict to create a great story. As the name suggests, it is the "one story" cycle: a universal template for story.

Secular author Robert McKee agrees. In his popular how-to book for screenwriters,[3] McKee strongly recommends that aspiring writers should mold their scripts according to this cycle. In his opinion, the more narrowly that a writer varies from this plot pattern, the more commercial success the writer is likely to experience. This classic understanding of story seems to be "hardwired" into the human psyche. "It is a mirror of the human mind. . . . It is neither ancient or modern, Western nor Eastern; it is human."[4] It represents the way that story works. Some of the most popular television programming has recognized and utilized this pattern. If you remember the old TV show *Murder, She Wrote,* you will already be familiar with this plot structure. This popular television series featured renowned actress Angela Lansbury, who played Jessica Fletcher.

Most of the weekly episodes followed the same basic plot. Here is my tongue-in-cheek encapsulation of a "typical" episode.

Back-Story

The back-story refers to the events that establish the circumstances and setting for the current story. Jessica Fletcher is a former substitute English teacher who left the classroom to become a famed mystery writer. She frequently finds her talents as a mystery writer used to solve the mysteries that arise in her small town of Cabot Cove, Maine.

Summer 1

This is a state of bliss — it is as wonderful as a summer vacation but as boring to watch as paint drying. In good stories, summer does not last long.

> **Scene 1**: A typical episode may open with a scene of Jessica having lunch in the tearoom with an old friend as they discuss an upcoming library fund-raising event.

Fall

Fall contains the scenes that move the plot away from the perfection of summer. The further events descend away from the initial perfection of summer, the greater the reader senses tension. Tension is the emotional discontinuity that readers feel when life is not what it should be. The interest of the audience increases as the tension increases. Most of the scenes (and chronological time) take place in fall. Note how each scene gradually increases the tension that the reader feels. The scenes are not random. Each one carefully and deliberately builds on what precedes it and contributes to what is ahead.

> **Scene 2**: Jessica walks out of the back door of the tearoom and trips over a body. Mary, a young woman in her twenties who worked at a local coffee shop, was stabbed to death a few hours before. *Clearly the perfection of summer has ended.*
>
> **Scene 3**: Mark, a distant relative of Jessica who came to Cabot Cove to find summer employment as a house painter, is implicated in the murder. This graduate medical student who does advanced cancer research in Boston during the school year was seen arguing with the deceased in the local coffee shop early that morning. *The*

tension is increasing. We don't want to see this young man wrongly accused of murder.

Scene 4: As the (inept) town sheriff does his investigation, he discovers that Mark and Mary had dated a few years previously. Could the embers of this old relationship have flared up again and resulted in murder? *The tension increases as the circumstantial evidence mounts. Have we found a motive for murder?*

Scene 5: The forensics report comes back from the lab. Traces of paint were found on the knife used to stab Mary. The paint on the handle is the same brand and color of paint that Mark has been using on his current painting job. The sheriff comes and leads Mark off to jail in handcuffs. "I'm sorry, Jessica. I know he's a relative of yours, but all the evidence points toward Mark. I have no choice but to arrest him." *The story keeps getting worse (colder). It is steadily descending toward winter.*

Scene 6: Jessica meets with Mark in his prison cell and Mark strongly asserts his innocence. "Yes, we used to be lovers. Yes, we argued that morning, but I did not kill her, Jessica. I didn't even know she lived here. You know me, Jessica. I could never do such a thing. All I want to do is to return to my research in Boston and cure cancer." *Jessica (and the viewer) are now convinced that Mark is telling the truth. But if Mark did not murder Mary, who did? The tension is increased as we become emotionally committed to Mark. We want him to cure cancer, but it looks like he is going to spend the rest of his life in prison. We have arrived in winter.*

Winter

This is a state of angst. In this stage, life is bleak and unbearable. It is the worst of all possible scenarios — what Shakespeare called the "winter of our discontent." Winter is as bad as life can be and the characters in the story (as well as the readers) despair that things may never improve. Winter is the crescendo of the events of fall. It is the apex of bad news. It takes a long time to get to winter, but we do not stay in winter long.

*Winter ends with a **surprising twist** in the plot. This is a completely unexpected development in the story that turns the story around. From this point on, circumstances in the story begin to improve. The surprising twist is the key to the story. It is the pivotal event that redeems a terrible situation.*

Scene 7: Jessica invites all of the key players in this episode to her home (and amazingly they all show up). Here she begins to review the evidence that had mounted against her nephew. "What surprised me about the key piece of evidence, the painty knife, was that there were no fingerprints. Why not, I wondered? So I asked an old friend at the lab to run some extra tests. What he found on the knife was a unique latex residue — the kind of latex used to make a brand of hygienic glove sold exclusively by a chain of paint stores in New England. A chain that has a store right here in Cabot Cove."

Jessica swings to face the paint store clerk named John and makes her accusation. "It was you, wasn't it? You have been infatuated with Mary and frustrated that she wouldn't respond to your advances. This morning when you witnessed the tension-filled exchange between Mark and Mary, you didn't just see an argument. You saw your opportunity. You quickly ran across the street to the paint store, put on latex gloves to hide your identity, and smeared some of the paint that you had just mixed for Mark on an old knife. After Mary spurned your advances one more time, you stabbed her to death behind the coffee shop, knowing that Mark would be implicated in her murder. John . . . how could you?"

John spontaneously and tearfully confesses.

This surprising twist in the plot removes all tension in the story. It resolves the ambiguity of the story. If the TV show began at 8:00 p.m., the twist would not take place until about 8:50. The plot of the story is driven by conflict. This conflict results in a feeling of tension in the audience. Tension keeps us watching. When the tension is resolved, the story is almost over. Almost. Only two things remain: spring and summer.

Spring

This is a good time. At this point in the story, you know that while not yet perfect, things are on their way back to bliss. The unexpected twist has changed everything. Winter's back is broken. Summer is just around the corner.

Scene 8: John is led to a waiting police car in handcuffs as townspeople look on in shock and dismay. Mark is welcomed back into respectability by the townspeople. New house painting clients step forward to help him earn the money he needs to go back to school in the fall and fight cancer. Everyone is happy. Spring has arrived. Summer is right around the corner.

Summer 2

We come back to where we began; a state of bliss.

Scene 9: For a brief moment we see Jessica smiling and laughing back in the tearoom with her old friend as they talk about the upcoming library fund-raiser. All is right with the world again.

Applying the Mono-Mythic Cycle to Scripture

The mono-mythic cycle may help us understand TV shows, but does it help us make sense of Scripture? Does it give a literary framework with which to interpret the biblical narrative? Let's see if we can apply it to the grand narrative of the Bible.

How does the story of Scripture begin?

Back-Story

Satan is the highest of God's created beings (see Isa. 14). In his pride, however, Satan seems to have wanted to exalt himself to the level of equality with God. God responded to this act of rebellion by casting him out of heaven. It would be safe to say that there was bad blood between God and Satan. This existing history is the larger context (back-story) of the Bible.

Summer 1

The story of Scripture begins in the Garden of Eden. It starts in bliss. Eden is wonderful. Eden is perfect. It is God (the protagonist) and humanity (God's most precious and loved creation) living in perfect harmony. Humanity and divinity walk together in the cool of the evening. The fellowship is intimate and unsullied. If you and I were Adam and Eve, we would never have wanted it to end. From a literary perspective, however, summer is boring. So how long does summer last in the Bible? Not long. The Fall happens in Genesis 3. And what comes next? The fall.

Fall

It does not take long for the antagonist, Satan, to show up in God's perfect world. Satan is as evil as God is good. And he is intent on destroying God's perfect world, including his most precious creation: humanity.

Scene 1:[5] Satan's impact is as devastating as it was disconcerting. With a few deft conversations, Adam and Eve eat the forbidden fruit and are expelled from the garden. *This is not good. Fall has arrived. Satan appears to be winning this contest. There is a chill in the air. This is the* **inciting event** *of the Bible's story.*

Scene 2: The first children enter into conflict. Cain murders his brother Abel. *The tension increases for the reader as Satan appears to be gaining the upper hand in God's world.*

Scene 3: World events continue to escalate out of apparent control as humanity became so corrupt that God seems forced to "hit the reset button" on his creation (in Gen. 6!) and sends a universal flood. *This is not good. Satan appears to be winning consistently.*

Scene 4: God chooses to work through the lineage of Abraham. To an outsider this could appear as if God has surrendered humanity to

Satan and is willing to be content with just one family. And how would you describe Abraham's ancestors? Functional or dysfunctional? Who appears to be winning this contest? God or Satan? The further things move away from ideal, the greater the tension we feel. And the more interesting the story becomes.

Scene 5: The people of Israel end up slaves for four hundred years and then wander around in the desert until an entire generation dies. God's people do not look impressive. *Satan appears to be winning the battle for humanity. The tension increases.*

Scene 6: When they finally make it into the Promised Land, they are ruled by judges. As a whole, would you view this leadership experiment a success or a failure? Then come the kings. David does fairly well, but most of the others are poor. After God destroys the northern kingdom because of their sin, you would think that the people of God would get their act together. Do they? No. They continue to sin, end up in Babylon, come back from their time of captivity, and go back into their sin. And then come the five hundred silent years. You know that things are not going well when God gives his people the silent treatment for five centuries. It almost appears that God has given up on humanity. *The tension continues to increase. We are beginning to despair if the situation will ever get better. Is it too far gone for even God to redeem?*

Scene 7: Readers who are ready to give up in despair at the end of the Old Testament have new hope with the dawning of the New Testament. Instead of giving up, God sends a champion — his only son, Jesus Christ. Boy, does this get our hopes up! He can do miracles and preach as no one before. It is quickly obvious that Jesus can do things that no other prophet before him could do. He has the potential to win a decisive victory over Satan! Victory is possible. We readers may not be eternally lost to Satan after all!

Winter

Scene 8: But then things begin to go wrong. Satan is not intimidated by Jesus. He manages to get Israel's religious leaders, who should have been his biggest supporters, to turn against him, as well as the general populace and the secular authorities. And even one of Jesus' inner circle, Judas, also joins the conspiracy. In fact, Satan is so successful that instead of Jesus being worshiped as king as he deserves, he is crucified between two common criminals. Jesus dies on the cross and goes to hell. Jesus, God's own son, has been defeated by Satan.

The story ends at the bottom of the mono-mythic cycle. It is a tragedy of unimaginable proportions. Satan has won. There is no hope for humanity on Good Friday. We are all lost. This is why the disciples begin to live life in the minor key after the crucifixion. They are discouraged and despondent. The reader knows that it will not take long for them to walk away from the occupied tomb and try to pick up the pieces of their shattered lives. Tension is at the maximum here. It cannot be increased. *This is winter. And the snow is ten feet deep! It is unbearable.*

Setback — this occurs when the protagonist suffers apparent defeat. All hope is lost. This is the dead of winter.

Unexpected Twist in the Plot

In all of literature, there is no more surprising plot twist than the resurrection of Jesus Christ. Can you imagine the scream that would have erupted from the pit of hell when Satan realized — too late — what had happened?

Scene 9: Satan had not outsmarted God after all. Just the reverse. In a move reminiscent of judo, God harnessed the momentum of Satan's evil actions to accomplish his holy purposes. While Satan was intentionally fulfilling his plan of killing the Son of God, he was also, unintentionally, carrying out God's eternal plan of salvation. As Satan pounded spikes into Jesus' innocent body, he was fulfilling God's eternal plan to use his Son as an atoning sacrifice for lost humanity. From the viewpoint of Easter, Calvary is not the site of evil's final victory. It is where God redeems his most precious creation with the blood of his Son. Humanity need not be enslaved by Satan for eternity. Salvation is available to all who trust in Jesus Christ alone for their salvation.

This surprising twist in the plot removes the tension from the story. God won. Victory is sure. The divine story is almost over. Only two things remain: spring and summer.

Spring

Scene 10: Pentecost takes place. The power of God's Holy Spirit is fully released. God does more than redeem his people. He empowers them. Joel's prophecy is fulfilled. We are living in a new day.

This is a happy time! The tension is almost entirely gone. The final consummation is almost upon us. Can't wait!

Scene 11: The growth of the church is wonderful! God is obviously not on the defensive. As a result of Christ's victory, the church begins to make enormous advances among Jew and Gentile alike!

Spring is getting warmer! It may not be summer yet, but we know it isn't far away.

Summer 2

Scene 12: The return of the king! Jesus Christ returns in the flesh as a triumphant king. All the enemies of Jesus are forced to bend the knee to him. And he not only judges the world as he sits on his great white throne, but transforms the entire planet. There is a new heaven and a new earth . . . which is even better than the original Garden of Eden. Moses could describe the original garden in the book of Genesis in physical terms. The apostle John cannot describe the new heaven and earth with the same terms. What is coming is so much better that John is forced to use metaphors as he tries to help us glimpse its grandeur.

In secular literature, the second summer is as good as the first summer. In biblical literature, however, the story usually ends up higher than it began. Things improve! Despite the long, long fall and the terrible agony of winter, we rejoice in the return of summer! The following diagram is probably a more accurate representation of biblical narrative.

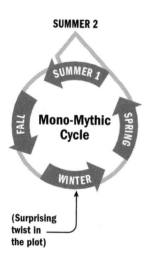

Smaller Mono-Mythic Cycles in Scripture

Understanding where the grand story of Scripture begins and ends is fairly easy: Genesis to Revelation. Understanding where the many smaller stories contained within the grand narrative start and stop, however, is not nearly as simple. You discover the circumference of a story by examining what the author is doing with the primary tension of the story in each scene. How does the original author use the scene to either increase or decrease the tension of the story? Drama is conflict — ordered conflict. It is the arrangement of consequential events for the communication of a central idea.

Scenes are like the individual pearls of a fine necklace. They are all attached to an organizing strand (plot). You need to ask yourself: "Where does this particular pearl fit?" Scenes do not have individual meaning. Each one uniquely contributes to a larger story. The question that the interpreter must ask is "how?" How does each individual scene contribute to the story as a whole? When you can trace the pearls from "Summer 1" to "Summer 2," the story is over.

In rare instances a story will not end in summer—there will not be a surprising twist in the plot. On these occasions, you have what literary scholars refer to as a tragedy. There are not many tragic stories in the Bible (Samson and Saul being two notable exceptions), but they do exist. Most of the stories of Scripture are comedies—not full of laughs, but comedic in a literary sense. They end by providing their audiences with a happy conclusion. They end back in "summer." The question to ask is: "How does each scene contribute to the overall structure of the story?"

To understand what is happening with each scene, I recommend that you use a Scene Analysis Chart (see appendix 2). To make sure that you properly understand the structure of the story, duplicate the attached chart found in the appendix and fill it out.

- At the *top* of each column write down the biblical reference of each paragraph of your story. (I find it helpful to follow the divisions of the NASB.)
- In the *large* portion of each column, jot down the significant exegetical observations you have made on each scene. As you do,
  - Look for the subtle clues (and occasional direct statements) that the narrator uses to make his point.
  - Take note of when the narrator picks up the pace of the story and when he slows it down. Narrators slow down to emphasize what is important to the story.
- In the *third section* of each column, write a brief descriptive summary of what happens in the scene. Summarize the action.
- Finally, at the *bottom* of each column indicate, first, the dramatic role that the original author intended for this scene to play. Which season is it? Second, outline how you think the author manages to increase or decrease the tension of the story within this scene. What happens to make you feel more or less anxious? Here are some elements to consider:
  - The solution to the problem of the story is found in the unexpected twist of the story. What happens here? How is the tension of the story relieved? What do you think the point of the story is?
  - Where do you think the story ends? Does this story have a happy ending, or is it a tragedy? Why?
  - Are there any obvious literary markers that confirm the beginning and end of this particular story?
  - Irony and poetic justice can confirm your understanding of the plot. If either is present in your story, they should be most visible in the "unexpected twist" of the plot.
  - Repetition can also confirm your understanding of the plot. Narrators sometimes use this to highlight their "big idea."

- Time is easily manipulated by narrators. They speed it up when dealing with less important events and slow it down to help us notice the critical elements. Where does the story slow down and why? Narrators may dechronologize events. Take note if you discover that events are presented in a different order than they have occurred historically. Why is this done? How does changing the chronology influence the meaning of the story?
- What do the characters say? Conversations are a favorite literary device used by narrators to powerfully and directly reveal the character of the individuals. What do the characters say? Why?
- Narrators will occasionally intertwine the plots of two related stories to communicate a single big idea. Is there a single problem being addressed by the author in two different ways?

Your goal here is to avoid the predicament pictured below by our good friend Calvin. What we want to do is "join the dots" that the ancient narrator has placed in the biblical story — to follow his literary clues. We want to discover the literary structure that was originally given to the biblical story, not impose our own. If we connect the dots of the story our own way — without regard for the purposes of the original author — we will end up drawing a picture for our congregations that God did not intend. Remember, a text cannot mean what it never meant. We must discover what a text meant before we can tell others what it means.

Calvin and Hobbes ©1992 Watterson. Reprinted with permission of Universal Press Syndicate. All rights reserved.

Before you move on, take a few minutes to put into practice what we have been talking about. Use a blank Scene Analysis Chart photocopied from appendix 2 and examine the structure of Daniel 1. Your goal is to utilize the dramatic tension of this story to determine where it begins and ends. (You cannot always trust chapter divisions; they are notoriously unreliable indicators of narrative structure.) After you have done this, compare your charts with the ones I have completed below. Please do not look at the completed charts until *after* you finish your work. Go ahead, give Daniel 1 a try.

Scene Analysis Chart

Passage	*Daniel 1:1–2*	*Daniel 1:3–5*

Exegetical observations	- Judah is captured by Babylon.
	- The narrator points out that the Lord gave
	  ○ Jehoiakim to Nebuchadnezzar
	  ○ some temple articles to Nebuchadnezzar.
	- It looks as if the narrator is hinting to the reader that God remains sovereign even when things seem to be going contrary to God's purposes.
		- An unprecedented opportunity is presented to some of Israel's elite young people; they can escape the devastation of their homeland and receive a full-ride scholarship (room and board!) for the best education available in the ancient world . . . with a career in the government of the world's greatest superpower waiting for them on graduation day.
		- Ashpenaz, chief of the court officials, was put in charge of this program by Nebuchadnezzar.

Summary: What happened? Recap the activity of this scene in one sentence.	Nebuchadnezzar (king of Babylon) conquers Judah.	Nebuchadnezzar introduces an education and career opportunity to the defeated and discouraged youth of Israel.
Dramatic purpose: • What did this scene accomplish for the overall story? • Is the tension increasing or decreasing? • How did the author manipulate the tension?	- This is the "back-story" of the narrative—here the narrator is placing the narrative in its historical context. - Daniel is a citizen of a small defeated nation that has been destroyed by war—his personal future is bleak.	- This is summer! Young people who once could only look ahead to a lifetime of survival existence are suddenly given the possibility of a wonderful future.

Daniel 1:6–7	Daniel 1:8–10	Daniel 1:11–14
- Daniel and his four friends are among the Israelites who pass the stringent entrance requirements! - Ashpenaz gives these successful applicants new names (the names of Babylonian gods).	- Daniel refuses to "defile" himself by eating the food and wine. Why? Two interpretive options. It may be an issue of eating nonkosher food or of eating food sacrificed to idols. Either way, it would be sinful to eat the meat. - God causes Ashpenaz to show favor and sympathy to Daniel. - Daniel asks Ashpenaz for permission not to eat the defiling food. - Ashpenaz sees this request as life threatening—for himself as well as for Daniel!	- Daniel goes behind Ashpenaz's back and makes the same food request to a guard (much lower on the administrative totem pole). - Daniel requests a ten-day trial that he promises will result in a dramatic physical transformation (this is a risky move—ten days is not much time for anyone to reap observable benefits from a new diet!). - The guard agrees (at obviously significant personal risk from offending both Ashpenaz and Nebuchadnezzar!).
Daniel and his friends receive the royal Babylonian scholarship and new Babylonian names.	Daniel's request to not defile himself with the royal repast is strongly rejected by Ashpenaz.	Daniel avoids defiling himself by getting the guard to agree to his desperate ten-day trial diet request.
- Fall has begun. The blissful joy of the scholarship has been tainted by the attempt of the chief official to change the names of Daniel and his friends. - Babylon will give Daniel and friends the wonderful future they want; all they need to do in return is to give passive allegiance to Babylonian gods!	Fall is getting colder here! The tension is increasing. Even though Ashpenaz *likes* Daniel, he will not agree to Daniel's plan. Ashpenaz thinks Daniel's plan is so dangerous that it could kill both of them!	This is winter. The tension is at a fever pitch. Daniel is not only putting his education and future career at risk here; he is also risking his life. The guard, Ashpenaz, or Nebuchadnezzar could have Daniel executed for his insubordination. His life is hanging by a proverbial thread. No matter what the cost, however, Daniel refuses to sin. He would rather die than sin.

Daniel 1:15–16	Daniel 1:17–20	Daniel 1:21
- It works! - At the end of the ten days, Daniel is observably healthier and better nourished than those who ate the defiling food! - The guard permanently alters their diet.	- God gives Daniel and his friends knowledge and understanding of literature and learning—Daniel can understand visions and dreams. - When Ashpenaz presents Daniel and friends at graduation, Nebuchadnezzar finds them ten times better than anyone else.	
Daniel and friends pass the test and their diet is permanently altered.	God rewards his undefiled servants beyond what they could have ever imagined.	Daniel remained in Babylon until King Cyrus.
The fact that the diet worked so well is the surprising twist in the story. The tension is gone. Spring is here. Things are getting better and better!	We are back in summer. These are the good days! In fact, the story ends higher than it began. Summer 1 was good, but Summer 2 is much better!	This statement has no dramatic influence on the story. This verse is a literary marker that provides secondary confirmation that the story has ended. In this case, chapter 1 is a complete story.

NOTES FOR CHAPTER THREE

1. Adele Berlin, *Poetics and Interpretation of Biblical Narrative* (Sheffield: Sheffield Academic Press, 1983), 125.
2. I am indebted to Dr. Reg Grant of Dallas Seminary for first introducing me to this concept.
3. Robert McKee, *Story* (New York: Regan, 1997).
4. Ibid., 62.
5. Additional scenes are representative rather than comprehensive.

WHAT COMES NEXT?
STEPS 4 THROUGH 8

Driving around Los Angeles is a nightmare. The city is so large and complex that during my recent move to the city, I found myself constantly getting lost. The detailed maps I displayed out across the front seat did not help. Only when I put away those neighborhood maps and purchased a one page map that gave me an overview of the entire city was I able to gain the perspective I needed. Too much detail too soon is confusing.

This is also true exegetically. As you have progressed through the preceding chapters, you have gained an overview of the narrative you want to preach. You understand its literary characteristics and broad historical context and you have identified its central idea. Now you are ready to zoom in on the details of the text.

 **Analyze the characters.**

The characters that populate the story are vital to the story itself. It is impossible to separate plot from character; they cannot exist independently. The character's actions drive the plot from scene to scene, and the plot's structure gives guidance to the actions of the character. Character is the rope that lashes a story together. You cannot understand a passage of narrative literature unless you understand the characters that walk across its scenes. The first step in understanding the characters in your story is to identify them.

What Do You Know about the Characters?

We have spent most of our academic lives trying to read faster and faster. When you are trying to get to know the characters of a biblical story, however, speed reading is not particularly helpful. S l o w d o w n! Take note of the character clues that the narrator has left for you in the biblical text. Here are some things to look for as you carefully study the characters in your story.

Contrast between characters. Is one character being utilized to highlight the characteristics of another? This is a common literary technique. You see this happening for example with Cain and Abel, Abraham and Lot, Jacob and Esau, and David and Saul. When you see this happening, ask yourself: "In what ways are these characters different? What is the narrator trying to highlight with this contrast?"

Comparison of characters. Sometimes the narrator chooses to arrange characters on the basis of similarity. In 1 and 2 Kings, for example, moral comparisons are frequently made between the kings of Israel and Judah as the dynasty is traced from Solomon to the time of the Exile. In 2 Chronicles comparisons are constantly made between those kings who patterned their lives after godly King David and those who did not.

Physical appearance. Our culture is obsessed with appearance. The biblical narrators are not. They seldom take the time to mention what a person looks like. When they do, however, take special note. These details are not given just to help you picture them more clearly. Physical details serve a variety of literary purposes.

- Physical attributes can advance the plot or explain its course. This is what happens in Genesis 27:11 when Jacob said to Rebekah his mother, "But my brother Esau is a hairy man, and I'm a man with smooth skin." This text explains how Jacob could impersonate his brother. Another example is Genesis 29:17: "Leah had weak eyes, but Rachel was lovely in form and beautiful." These physical details help explain why Jacob loved Rachel.

  In 2 Samuel 14:25 Absalom's beauty is described in some detail: "In all Israel there was not a man so highly praised for his handsome appearance as Absalom. From the top of his head to the sole of his foot there was no blemish in him." The verses that follow make much of his hair and Absalom's vanity surrounding it. Later events reveal the important role that Absalom's vanity and hair played in his downfall.

- Physical attributes can emphasize a character's emotions. Nehemiah's love for his homeland was expressed physically in Nehemiah 2:2 when "the king asked me, 'Why does your face look so sad when you are not ill? This can be nothing but sadness of heart.'"

- Clothing can advance the plot. In Genesis 38:14, Tamar, Judah's daughter-in-law, "took off her widow's clothes, covered herself with a veil to disguise herself, and then sat down at the entrance to Enaim, which is on the road to Timnah. For she saw that, though Shelah had now grown up, she had not been given to him as his wife." This explains why Judah did not recognize her by the side of the road.

  In Joshua 9:4–5 the Gibeonites used clothing to stage a ruse that fooled the Israelites: "They went as a delegation whose donkeys were loaded with worn-out sacks and old wineskins, cracked and mended. The men put worn and patched sandals on their feet and wore old clothes. All the bread of their food supply was dry and moldy."

Inner character. There are occasions when it is easy to determine the inner character of an individual. On these occasions we are told directly by a trustworthy individual and no interpretation is necessary. Sometimes God tells us directly about the heart of a character, as in Job 1:8: "Then the LORD said to Satan, 'Have you considered my servant Job? There is no one on earth like him; he is blameless and upright, a man who fears God and shuns evil.'" On other occasions, it is the narrator who tells us clearly (and correctly) about a person's character. In Genesis 6:9, for example, we learn from the narrator that "Noah was a righteous man, blameless among the people of his time, and he walked with God." And in 1 Samuel 2:12, "Eli's sons were wicked men; they had no regard for the LORD."

Interpretive caution should be employed, however, when one personality in a story refers to the inner character of another individual. Sometimes this characterization is correct, but not always. Be careful not to accept every comment at face value. Similar caution needs to be employed when characters refer to themselves.

The most common way for narrators to disclose the inner character is simply to present the individual in action. This is the staple of biblical narrative and the building blocks of plot. Character is revealed through actions. The best way to gain insight into a person's inner character is to watch them.

The importance of the commonplace. People's daily lives are seldom mentioned, so give uncommon attention to the commonplace when studying biblical narratives. The author will be using that seemingly mundane detail to achieve his purposes. For example, in Genesis 25:34 we read: "Then Jacob gave Esau some bread and some lentil stew. He ate and drank, and then got up and left. So Esau despised his birthright." The narrator is using the common occurrence of eating to show that Esau valued his stomach over his birthright. The addition of this detail helps us "see" the point that the narrator is making. We gain the same kind of vivid insight into the calloused hearts of Joseph's brothers when they sit down to eat immediately after stripping him of his robe and throwing him into an abandoned cistern (Gen. 37:23–25).

Repeated actions. The more often a person exhibits the same behavior, the more he or she confirms character traits. We know that Samson had a significant problem with his sexuality because he succumbs twice to this particular temptation. Repetition also reveals that Job is a particularly righteous man when in Job 1:5 we read: "Early in the morning he would sacrifice a burnt offering for each of them, thinking, 'Perhaps my children have sinned and cursed God in their hearts.' This was Job's regular custom."

What is your goal in this character analysis? You should "view yourself as the observant traveling companion of the characters in a story (especially the protagonist) and simply get to know the characters as thoroughly as the details allow you to do."[1]

To help you accomplish this task I recommend that you use the Character Identification Sheet found in appendix 3.

- In the far left column, simply write down a character's name.
- In the next column, jot down any details that the biblical narrator provides about the characters. Are you told how fat/rich/noble/ordinary they are? Write down everything that the biblical narrator wants you to know about these people.
- In the next column, write what they do. Actions speak louder than words. They reveal character.
- Next, write down what motivation the characters have to act the way they do. Nobody acts without a reason. Only animals respond with pure instinct. To varying degrees, we all have reasons for what we do. Why do these characters choose to act as they do? What was their motivation?
- In the final column, think about how these characters feel. Imagine the emotion that they must have experienced as they go through the various scenes of your story. Empathize with them.

Once you have identified the individual characters, you need to determine the role the narrator intends for these characters to play. What is their literary purpose? I recommend that you classify the characters into one of three categories: protagonist, antagonist, or foil.

Identity of the Main Characters

The Protagonist

Protagonists are the dominant characters of a story (whether positive or negative). They are willful individuals working hard to create a conscious desire into reality. We may not always like the protagonist, but they will always be people we can identify with. Deep within the protagonist, we sense a shared humanity. We may not agree with their goal but we know why they want to achieve it. They are like us. As a result, we instinctively want them to succeed. We feel a shared kinship.

This identification is the basis of our emotional identification with the protagonists. It is the reason why we cry if they fail and cheer if they succeed. Protagonists are typically the only ones in a story who experience "arc" (significant character development) as the story moves towards resolution. They grow toward or away from God's ideal through the choices they make and the events that take place in the narrative. Biblical narrators typically use protagonists to embody their "big idea." They show us how we should or should not live.

> Every story has a central character. This is simply one of the principles of selectivity and emphasis that storytellers impose on their material. The central character is called the protagonist. . . . Stories are built around the protagonist.[2]

The Antagonist

Antagonists make stories interesting because they are the primary source of conflict. An antagonist is the one character of a story who provides the primary opposition for the protagonist. The greater the opposition that the antagonist generates, the greater the audience interest produced. Antagonists try to prevent protagonists from accomplishing their goals. They are more powerful than the protagonist is. A good antagonist will use available resources to drive the protagonist to the very edge of catastrophe.

The protagonist can only be as compelling as the antagonist forces him to be. The antagonist will not usually experience personal growth or development (character arc) in a story. If an antagonist triumphs, the story is tragedy (it ends in winter). If the antagonist is finally defeated, the story is a comedy (ends back in summer).

The Foils

Foils are the lesser characters of the story that are necessary to advance the plot but do not occupy a dramatically significant role in the story. They are the bit actors in the major Hollywood motion pictures. In the original *Star Trek* TV series, the foils were often the red-shirted crewmembers. These anonymous people beamed down to a planet only to be quickly eaten by a rock monster. The only literary purpose they served was to demonstrate that rock monsters were dangerous creatures. They were expendable crewmembers. They were foils.

Literary foils are similar to the silver umbrellas used by professional portrait photographers. The purpose of those silver umbrellas is not to attract attention to themselves. In fact, it would be a mistake to include the umbrellas in the main picture. Their only purpose is to reflect light on the main characters of the photograph. Foils are to narratives what silver umbrellas are to photography. They set off or heighten another character.

In-Depth Analysis

Once you know who the protagonist and antagonist are in your story, you need to get to know them in detail. You need to dig as deeply into their personalities as you possibly can. Get to know them as intimately as the text will allow.

Motivation

People are what they do, not what they say. Who we are is revealed when we are under pressure. The pressures of life shape and reveal our values. Values are the beliefs and ideas that shape our decisions.

People tend to choose the path of least resistance. No one will deliberately make his or her life more difficult than necessary. So why do your characters tolerate (and not flee) the conflict of the passage? Because of their values. Your protagonist may value honesty. Your antagonist may hunger for power. The way that they respond to the stimuli of events is determined by the values that they hold.

The sum of a person's values is that person's character. The pressures of life reveal our true values and character. Do you think people should tell the truth? Would you tell the truth even if it cost you your job? What about if it cost you your entire career? What about if it cost you your family? Your life? Your true values are only revealed by pressure. Any boat will float in the harbor on a calm Sunday morning. Only the sturdiest of ships can stay the course in the midst of a "category four" hurricane. The only way to know the true character of someone is to "test their mettle," to see how they perform under tremendous pressure. Just ask Job.

> True character is revealed in the choices a human being makes under pressure — the greater the pressure, the deeper the revelation, the truer the choice to the character's essential nature.[3]

You will not understand the protagonist or antagonist unless and until you understand the values that propel them through their story — values that become clearer as the pressure increases and that become most evident in the dead of winter, just before the unexpected twist in the plot.

Don't overlook motivation. There is a reason why the characters make the choices they do. If you don't know what their reasons are, then you don't understand the story. And you cannot preach a narrative you do not understand.

Identification

Look at these characters through the lens of your own life. Begin to relate on an emotional and psychological level.

- Is your character selfish? Do you remember a time when you were motivated to act selfishly? What did that feel like? How did that influence your choices?
- Is your character materialistic? Can you recall a time in your life when you wanted something (a car, a house, a book, etc.) more than anything else in life? What went through your mind? What options did you begin to consider? What compromises were you prepared to make?

You do not want to read your own life into the biblical text. What you do want to do, however, is to truly empathize with the characters. You may not agree with them, but you must understand them.

Consider Eli in 1 Samuel 2. The narrator tells us that his two boys were "wicked men" who slept with the women who served at the entrance to the Tent of Meeting. Even worse, they treated the Lord's offering with contempt. In 1 Samuel 2:22 Eli "heard about everything his sons were doing to all Israel." Since Eli occupied the offices of judge as well as high priest, it was clearly his responsibility to deal with his sons. The law was equally clear that the sons deserved execution. Yet, in verses 23–25 we read that Eli decided to just give them a good lecture! It is easy to be rough on ole Eli. But if you simply dismiss him as a disobedient old man, you will miss out on the power of the passage. Yes, Eli was wrong. The rest of the chapter makes this very clear. But he was a father! These are his boys!

How would any parent respond to the knowledge that God wanted you to execute your sons? I have two boys. I love my boys, Nathan and Jonathan. I remember when they entered the world. My oldest son, Nathan, was born on my thirtieth birthday. I remember the doctor asking me to cut the umbilical cord. I remember the first time I held Nathan: red, wrinkled, and ugly. As I held him in my arms, I turned away and began to weep. I wept because I knew that life would never be the same and that God had entrusted me with an awesome responsibility.

I love my boys. I am sure that Eli did as well. I also wonder about Eli's wife. We do not know anything about her, but he must have had one. Could it be that she died in childbirth? And that these boys were the last living link he had with the woman he loved? How could he kill these boys?

I am not trying to excuse Eli. His values were clearly out of whack. He was wrong for not honoring God above his family. The enormous pressure of that moment revealed who he really was, and God was right to remove him from office. But true exegesis will seek to understand the heart of a character. It will not be satisfied with a bloodless evaluation of textual data. It goes beyond a *Hawaii Five-O* "Just the facts, ma'am" approach to the text. It realizes that these were real flesh-and-blood people and asks the question, "How must they have *felt* during this episode?"

STEP FIVE | Discover the setting of the story.

Geography

Historical narratives do not take place in a vacuum. They occur in specific locations, and these locations have influence on the events of these stories. That's because, to a certain degree, our lives are influenced by our geography.

I recently moved from Boston, Massachusetts, to Los Angeles, California. I can attest that geography influences life. Last fall I was busy winterizing my home and raking mountains of leaves. This fall I could (if I knew how) go surfing down at Huntington Beach.

The stories of our lives are influenced by geography. Get a topographic map and study where your biblical story is taking place. How far do your characters journey? Was it uphill or downhill? What time of year is it? What kind of weather are they likely experiencing? What kind of animals or people groups are they likely to have encountered? Do not ignore the physical setting of your narrative, especially if it is referred to by the narrator.

Culture

All people have an ethnic heritage and social background. They also have religious and educational backgrounds. All characters have educational backgrounds. How is your character unique? How do these factors influence your story? Are there any social practices that inform your story? Do the necessary research.

I have found it helpful, for example, to purchase a number of books on shepherding in order to familiarize myself with that occupation. I grew up in the city. My only exposure to real sheep came a few years ago when I was driving with my family and happened to pass a flock grazing by the side of the road. I stopped and got the kids out of the back seat to go see real live sheep. They were so close to the roadside fence we could put our hand in and touch them. My sons caressed the sheep without a problem. As soon as I reached out my hand, however, the sheep sneezed. And, yes, I found myself covered with sheep snot. Other than wearing sweaters, this is as close as I have ever come to a sheep. I have no desire to come any closer. But I know that I will never understand shepherds until I know something about shepherding. I need to learn. Like you, I have to do my cultural research.

STEP SIX | State the "big idea" of the narrative.

The Exegetical Idea

At this point in the exegetical process, you have done a considerable amount of work in the text. You have amassed a huge amount of data. It is easy to become overwhelmed by all that you have done. You would not be the first preacher buried alive under an avalanche of information.

The homiletical danger of information overload is twofold. First, you begin to lose sight of the focus of the passage. This makes it impossible to create a sermon that has a clear point. With Sunday looming, however, you know that you have to preach something. This feeling of desperation makes it easy to succumb to the second danger of information overload: the information dump — that is, trying to compensate with quantity what you lack in clarity. We have all done this on occasion and discovered that it doesn't work.

Haddon Robinson is correct when he says that "mist in the pulpit is fog in the pew." If you are not sure what you are saying, the people will not have a clue what you are talking about. Effective preaching is clear preaching. It begins by stating the single idea of a natural unit of Scripture with laserlike precision and then focusing that idea on the lives of our listeners. Fashioning that sentence is as critical as it is difficult. It is the goal of our exegesis. As John Henry Jowett, a fine preacher of a previous generation, said so well:

> No sermon is ready for preaching, nor ready for writing out, until we can express its theme in a short, pregnant sentence as clear as crystal. I find the getting of that sentence the hardest, the most exacting, and the most fruitful labour in my study. To compel oneself to fashion that sentence, to dismiss every word that is vague, ragged, ambiguous, to think oneself through to a form of words which defines the theme with scrupulous exactness — this is surely one of the most vital and essential factors in the making of a sermon: and I do not think any sermon ought to be preached or even written, until that sentence has emerged clear as a cloudless moon.[4]

You need to crystallize what you have learned — synthesize the author's central idea from the mountain of detail you have amassed. You need to state clearly the single idea that the original author intended to communicate to the original recipients of this story. You must press on beyond content to intent.

How do we accomplish this task? How do we avoid being buried by our own exegesis? *By stating the big idea of the text in the form of an exegetical subject and complement.*

A subject should answer the question, "What is this text talking about?" And it should always be written out in the form of a question. The complement provides the answer to this question. It completes the thought. If the subject of a passage was, "Why should Christians pray?" the complement could be, "Christians should pray because prayer will enrich their relationship with God." There is only one subject for every natural unit of Scripture. While some types of literature (such as epistles) allow for multiple complements, narratives do not. The stories of Scripture have only one subject and complement. Again, the first thing you want to do is to state the exegetical idea of the text.

An exegetical idea must be as close to the biblical text as possible. It is an accurate descriptive summary of what took place in the narrative. Your exegetical idea will probably have the names of dead people in it. It will have the smell of the ancient world about it. That's OK. What you are striving for here is accuracy. What do exegetical ideas look like? Here are a couple of examples of exegetical ideas based on what we have done in the previous chapter.

Daniel 1 — Exegetical Idea
Subject: What happened when Daniel and his friends refused to defile themselves by consuming the royal food and wine?
Complement: God gave them better health and academic success than all of the students who ate the defiling food.

The entire story of Scripture — Exegetical Idea
Subject: How did God restore sinful humanity to himself?
Complement: Through the death and resurrection of Jesus Christ.

I am not trying to be cute or clever as I write these exegetical ideas. My sole goal is textual accuracy. How can we be sure that we have discovered the correct exegetical idea? I recommend that you use the metaphor of a wagon wheel pictured below.

Fashioning the "Big Idea"

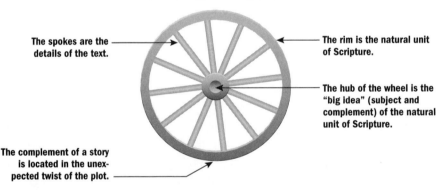

The spokes are the details of the text.

The rim is the natural unit of Scripture.

The hub of the wheel is the "big idea" (subject and complement) of the natural unit of Scripture.

The complement of a story is located in the unexpected twist of the plot.

The rim of the wagon wheel represents the natural unit of Scripture. You cannot find the big idea if you have not properly located the beginning and end of your story. You must know where the narrative starts and stops. The spokes of the wheel represent the details of the story, which you have discovered during your exegesis. The hub of the wheel represents the big idea of the passage. You can be sure that you have identified the correct big idea if every spoke attaches to the hub, that is, if your subject and complement embrace all of the details of the passage. No textual spokes are left dangling. If your idea sounds good but does not explain two or three details of the text, then you do not have the right big idea. You are close, but not close enough. I find myself making half a dozen attempts at writing out the subject and complement of a passage before I form one that fits right in the middle of the wagon wheel — connects with every single spoke. I have also found that when I scribble my attempts out on a piece of paper, it is easier for me to go back and use elements from my inadequate ideas to fashion the accurate idea.

As challenging as identifying the exegetical idea may be, the mono-mythic cycle makes this task much easier for narrative literature. How? Because you will always find the complement at the "unexpected twist" in the plot. The element in the story that turns the narrative back to summer is the key to the passage. It answers the question posed by the subject. The surprising death and resurrection of Jesus Christ is the answer to the question: How will God restore sinful humanity to himself? The complement lives in the unexpected twist of your story.

Homiletical Idea

A homiletical idea is almost identical to the exegetical idea. The only difference is that it has been rewritten into eternal terms. It becomes an idea that transcends the specifics of any one time and culture. This idea will not contain the names of dead people or ancient places. While it will remain essentially the same as the exegetical idea, the homiletical idea will be understandable and applicable to a twenty-first-century audience. We can refashion the exegetical idea of Daniel 1 as follows:

Daniel 1 — Homiletical Idea
Subject: What happens when God's people refuse to allow their culture to pressure them into sin?
Complement: God will honor them for their faithfulness.

The entire story of Scripture — Homiletical Idea
Subject: How can we enjoy a restored relationship with God?
Complement: Through the death and resurrection of Jesus Christ.

Preaching Idea

The preaching idea is a pithy, memorable phrase that you want to lodge in the minds of your listeners. These are to preaching what bumper stickers are to driving: memorable, nutshell expressions of truth that adhere to your mind like white dog hair to your black dress pants. Preaching ideas are not nearly as comprehensive as your exegetical or homiletical ideas. On their own, they may not even make sense to people who did not hear your sermon. But for those who heard the message, the preaching idea can be a helpful long-term memory tool. It can nail the biblical idea deep into the minds and lives of your listeners.

Daniel 1 — Preaching Idea
God comes through!

The entire story of Scripture — Preaching Idea
The ticket home.

STEP SEVEN | Double-check your big idea.

Ideas are extraordinarily powerful. They shape our lives. We are a sum of our core convictions. This is why good preaching is so vital to the health of God's people. If we preach God's ideas, we will bring life and health to his people. If, however, we use our pulpit to say in God's name that which God did not say, we are like the false prophets of Jeremiah's day who "speak visions from their own minds, not from the mouth of the LORD" (Jer. 23:16). This is why James warned: "Not many of you should presume to be teachers, my brothers, because you know that we who teach will be judged more strictly" (James 3:1).

It is critical that God's spokespeople only speak God's ideas, because a teacher's words are like bits in the mouths of horses, rudders on ships, and small sparks in a great forest. They have enormous influence on the lives and destinies of others. Wrong ideas can wreak enormous and eternal havoc. It is critical that we only say from the pulpit what God has said in his Word. For this reason, I ask that you double-check the big idea you have so diligently developed. Make sure that it is the word of God. Submit your idea to the following questions.

- *Does your big idea make sense out of every part of the story?* Do all the "spokes" of the text connect to your big idea? If you think you have figured out Jonah but do not know what to do with chapter 4, you do not yet have the big idea.
- *Does your big idea fit easily into the context?* Epic literature (large narrative books such as Acts, Samuel, and Chronicles) is one large story made up of numerous smaller stories. These smaller stories all contribute to the one large story of the book. How does the idea you are suggesting fit into the grand story of the entire book? Small stories of epic literature are individual puzzle pieces. Does your proposed idea "snap into place" with the surrounding pieces? This is easier to do if you are preaching a series of messages through a single book.
- *Does your big idea fit through the filter of systematic theology?* While many different human writers wrote the Bible, it has a literary coherence. It was all inspired by God. The literary implication of this unified authorship is biblical coherence. God does not say one thing in one book and then contradict himself in another. The Bible enjoys

a wonderful unity. Systematic theologians have understood this unity and used it to weave the Bible's individual truths into a single coherent fabric of truth. Their work is of enormous benefit to you as a preacher. If you come up with a "big idea" that is out of step with the teaching of Scripture as a whole, you need to recheck your exegesis. God does not contradict himself.

- *Does your big idea have an explosive force to it?* This is a subjective way of asking the systematic theology question above. Can you visualize yourself standing in the pulpit communicating it to your congregation? Does the truth of this passage make you excited about the possibility of preaching it, or do you, as a seasoned minister, feel some pastoral apprehension? This hesitation may be of the Holy Spirit. If you sense this, ask the questions above once more. As responsible shepherds of God's flock, we want to be sure that we do not say anything that may harm the flock.

STEP EIGHT | Make the application.

One of the distinguishing marks of a sermon is that its purpose is to make a concrete behavioral change in the lives of the listeners. No sermon recorded in Scripture was ever preached for the sole purpose of increasing the information base of the audience. A sermon is not a lecture. It is not primarily interested in communicating content. The goal of a sermon is always to effect change in the lives of those listening. Information is a tool used to influence conduct. Sermons that touch the minds but bypass the lives of the listeners are bad sermons.

One of the most common evangelical approaches to narrative application has been allegory. Many well-meaning preachers, unaware of narrative literary structure, have gone to extraordinary and even fanciful lengths to apply narrative texts. In an excellent article entitled "The Problem with Allegory in Preaching," David E. Reid recounts an evangelistic sermon he heard from Genesis 24:63–64 that contained the following applications:[5]

1. The camel's nose detects water from far away and enables it to lead its rider to a place in the desert where he may drink. *God's grace can lead thirsty seekers to spiritual water.*
2. The camel's hooves are such that they will not sink in the sand. *Grace keeps God's people from sinking in the sin of the world.*
3. The camel's kneecaps allow him to kneel so a rider can dismount and hide behind the camel during a sandstorm. *Grace shields us during the storms of life.*

4. The camel's teeth can bite into cactus and eat its meat without getting stuck by its thorns, which symbolize the curse. *Grace allows hungry seekers to receive spiritual food in a sinful world.*
5. The camel's humped back is ridiculed as being ugly, but it carries supplies that meet people's needs. *The world ridicules God's grace, but grace meets our needs.*
6. The camel's saddlebags carry healing balms, treasure, and fruit. *God's grace heals us, provides for us, and sustains us.*
7. The camel is unattractive in appearance but of great importance for those who live in the desert. *God's grace expressed in Christ on the cross was not a pretty sight, but it is precious to those who trust him.*

This is *not* an example to follow. Stories do not have points. They have a point. Narratives are organized around a single controlling idea to achieve a single purpose in the lives of the listeners. Do not try to locate multiple significances or applications from a single story. Just get the point and drive it home. Here are some questions to help you properly apply a narrative text.

1. *What is the central principle espoused in this passage?* The core principle of Daniel 1 is the steadfast refusal to sin despite the enormous pressure of an ungodly culture.
2. *What would this story look like if it were updated to the twenty-first century?* In an updated setting, this story could feature a female Christian Ph.D. history student from Sudan studying on a full scholarship at Harvard. This young woman feels understandably vulnerable living in a strange country and cold culture on the strength of a student visa. The situation becomes desperate, however, when her doctoral advisor starts pressuring her to write a dissertation that falsely chastises the Christian church for its influence on Africa through the centuries. If she refuses, she may lose her advisor's support to continue in the program and forfeit her visa. (By rewriting the issue in a contemporary setting, you improve your understanding of the central issues of the text. You are forced to distinguish between the temporal and eternal elements of the text.)
3. *In what way would your life (and those who will hear this message) change if you learned and applied the lesson of this story?* On a personal level, our faith would grow deeper and bolder. On an interpersonal level, we would discover that our actions resulted in a broad witness among unbelievers and an encouragement for fellow believers.
4. *In what way would your life (and those who will hear this message) change if you ignored the lesson of this text?* Choosing to ignore the lesson of this text would lead to short-term career advancement. We

would also betray our God, greatly diminish our ability to act as salt and light in an evil society, and set a negative example for our fellow believers.

By asking these questions, you will be better able to focus your application emphasis on the main point of the text and then to apply it with relevance to the lives of your listeners.

Congratulations

Congratulations! You have now successfully completed the first essential task of the biblical preacher. You have exegeted the narrative passage that you will be preaching. Do you think that this exegesis was an awful lot of work? You are right. But take heart. That central idea you have crafted is worth more than its weight in gold. It is the key to an effective sermon. You will find that when you invest the time and energy necessary to do good narrative exegetical work, you make the homiletical task far easier. You have made significant strides toward the construction of an effective first-person biblical sermon. Now let's cross over to the homiletical element of the preaching task. Let's finish the job. Let's write an effective first-person sermon!

NOTES FOR CHAPTER FOUR

1. Leland Ryken, *Words of Delight: A Literary Introduction to the Bible* (Grand Rapids: Baker, 1987), 75.
2. Leland Ryken, *How to Read the Bible as Literature* (Grand Rapids: Zondervan, 1984), 43.
3. Robert McKee, *Story* (New York: Regan, 1997), 101.
4. John Henry Jowett, *The Preacher, His Life and Work* (New York; Doran, 1912), 133.
5. David E. Reid, "The Problem with Allegory in Preaching," *Preaching Magazine* (November–December 1995), 68ff.

PART TWO

STEPS IN THE HOMILETICAL TASK

Chapter Five

TAKING THE FIRST STEPS IN THE HOMILETICAL TASK

Comedian Rodney Dangerfield made a career out of complaining: "I don't get no respect." Narrative preachers could say the same thing. Good stories fit together so naturally and a good storyteller relates them so effortlessly that they seem easy to do. They aren't. Try it. I have taken a perverse pleasure through the years in watching young seminary students learn this lesson.

I have had the privilege of teaching some of the brightest men and women at some of North America's finest theological institutions. When they come to campus, they often arrive with stratospheric GPAs and a corresponding intellectual disrespect for narrative literature. When I give the assignment of retelling one of Jesus' parables in contemporary garb, some of these young intellectuals respond with contempt. They leave class thinking they have just received a "Sunday school" level assignment. How hard can a story be?

This attitude encourages them to leave the assignment to the last minute. Many try to prepare their story the night before it is due. What their bloodshot eyes and nervous demeanor reveal the following morning, however, is that Jesus was smarter than they gave him credit for. Telling the dynamic equivalent of Jesus' stories — ensuring that your

©1992 Joe Martin. Reprinted with permission. All rights reserved.

story makes exactly the same point and emotional impact as the original — is not easy! Neither is creating an effective first-person expository sermon.

Creating narrative sermons that convey exactly the same idea and emotional impact as a biblical story is harder than it looks. It requires far more than neatness. But it is possible. Here's how to do it.

STEP ONE | Select an appropriate text.

Begin by selecting a natural unit of Scripture. For narrative literature, this means selecting an entire story. It is impossible to preach a fragment of a story. Individual scenes are meaningless. They become meaningful when attached to the rest of the story. The development of an effective narrative sermon begins by selecting a whole story from the pages of Scripture.

This principle is violated with alarming regularity. It is not unusual for preachers to try and preach a single scene or try and stretch a single story into a seven-week sermon series. Don't do this. Your goal as a preacher is to homiletically harness the natural dramatic tension of your narrative as it crescendos toward its climax. If you do not have a complete story, you will have insufficient tension, no big idea, and no resolution — satisfying or otherwise. You will end up with a boring, substandard sermon. It is impossible to preach an effective expository sermon unless you begin with a natural unit of Scripture — an entire story.

This task is more difficult to accomplish when you are working with New Testament literature. The gospels contain some of Scripture's most homiletically challenging narrative literature. The narrative books of the Old Testament are far more consistent in genre than the gospels. The gospels are constantly moving in and out of genre; they are a marvelous mosaic of literary styles. For this reason, I find the gospels to be the most exhilarating and demanding literature to preach. They are not pure narrative. Keep this in mind when you are selecting an appropriate passage for a first-person sermon. You cannot create a powerful first-person sermon if you do a poor job identifying the natural unit of Scripture.

This does not mean, however, that you should preach all of the stories you find in Scripture in the first-person. First-person sermons are only one of many homiletical options available to the preacher. First-person sermons are a legitimate way to preach narrative literature, but they are not the only way. The strength of the first-person homiletical rests in its unsurpassed ability to communicate emotion. You may want to consider other sermonic options when the biblical narrative you are exegeting is not overflowing with dramatic action.

There is nothing more inspiring than hearing a person relate a personal traumatic event. Humanity has an insatiable thirst for dramas "based on a true story." But not every day of our life contains material suitable for the "movie of the week." Most days are comprised of the mundane and the trivial. Quite forgettable. This does not mean that those days were not significant, just not particularly dramatic.

In the same way the stories of Scripture, while equally inspired, are not equally riveting. The wise preacher will select only the most emotion-filled and action-packed stories to preach in the first person. The inherent advantages of first-person sermons are best leveraged when they are paired with biblical stories pulsating with emotion. Stirring, action-packed stories beg for first-person treatment.[1] Don't preach them just to be cute or cutting edge. The only legitimate reason to preach a first-person sermon is that it is the best way to communicate the truth of a passage.

 STEP TWO | # Ensure that you have identified the "big idea" of your narrative.

As with "regular" sermons you must begin by identifying the subject and complement of the passage. This is not just good theology. It is good storytelling. Robert McKee warns Hollywood scriptwriters that "the more ideas you try to pack into a story, the more they implode upon themselves, until the film collapses into a rubble of tangential notions saying nothing."[2]

It is critical that you have thought your text through to absolute clarity. If you do not know precisely what the biblical writer said in your passage to the original audience, you will not be able to write an effective first-person sermon. Write out your exegetical, homiletical, and preaching ideas on a yellow post-it note and stick it to the top corner of your computer screen. Don't let anything you write deflect you from your goal of communicating this idea. Remember, you want to communicate intent, not just content!

STEP THREE | # Develop the protagonist for your story.

The protagonist is the central character of your story. He or she will be the driving force of the action of the story and the living embodiment of the big idea. You cannot develop the details of your first-person sermon until you have identified your protagonist. This may seem surprising. After all, shouldn't the protagonist of the biblical narrative automatically become the protagonist of your sermon? Not necessarily. As preacher, you have the option of choosing an entirely different character from the story. You also may decide to create a brand new character through whom to speak your story.

This advice may surprise you. "After all," you may object, "I believe that the biblical text is inspired and inerrant in every way. If the original coauthors of this story, human and divine, believe that their inscripturated story was the best way to write this story, then who are we to tamper with it? Is this right? Is it biblical? Surely our high view of Scripture ensures that we do not alter the biblical story in any way — that we would be most faithful to God and the text if we simply 'reran' the original story. Right?" I don't think so. Let me explain why.

I think that Abraham was a highly intelligent man. Suppose, however, I found a way to transport you and me, a TV, a DVD player, and Honda generator back to Abraham's day. As we meet with Abraham, we suggest that he watch a great movie we brought along. As I push the DVD into place, the movie flickers and begins. It is a Western.

The opening scene pans Main Street. The dirt road is lined on both sides with wooden sidewalks and clapboard buildings peeling white paint. Above the various doorways are signs saying "Sheriff," "Hotel," "General Store," and "Saloon." The saloon has those swinging shuttered doors incapable of keeping out either people or prairie dust. From inside the saloon you can hear the unmistakable sound of a player piano and the clinking of whiskey glasses. A few men are leaning against a hitching post smoking a cigarette as they wait for the stagecoach.

Out of the saloon walks Bart, an ugly man with a bad beard. He is wearing a black hat and vest. He has a huge wad of chewing tobacco in his mouth and a pair of revolvers hanging around his waist. He slowly walks down Main Street to the base of the clock tower and turns around. Out of the sheriff's office walks a man named Dan. Dan is clean shaven, wears a white hat, and sports a silver star on his chest. We notice the two pearl-handled revolvers on his waist as he walks straight down Main Street toward Bart. Dan stops when he is about twenty-five feet from Bart. We watch them stare at each other with their hands twitching just above their guns. The clock strikes noon.

I know that you understand the movie we just watched, but how would Abraham have understood? Not much. What would you have to explain? Electronic technology aside, you would have to explain the significance of black and white, what the star signified, what guns are, what a clock is, etc., etc., etc. If Abraham is so smart, why wouldn't he understand such an obvious movie? The story is obvious to us because it comes out of our contemporary culture. It builds on the myths that we grew up with, a central part of our cultural heritage. All narratives, including Western movies, build up — and assume — the cultural awareness of its audience. If you do not share the knowledge base of the original audience, you will not be able to fully appreciate the literature it generated, no matter how smart you are.

For Abraham to understand and appreciate this Western film the way that its original creator intended him to, the film would have to be modified significantly. How could you and I modify this film so that Abraham would understand and appreciate it as much as we do? To communicate the additional information that Abraham requires we would have to introduce new characters as well as add to and rearrange the original scenes. Perhaps we would have two children walking up Main Street talking about what guns do and how dangerous they are. And a couple of housewives buying groceries in the general store would reflecting on how good it is to know that the man who wears the star — the sheriff — is a good man whose job is to keep the town safe from evil people like Bart. And a bartender grows increasingly nervous as he sees noon drawing near, because "this is when business gets done, and only one man is coming back."

The changes I have suggested would significantly change the movie that the original director created. But the alterations I have suggested would not harm the director's original intention for the movie. On the contrary, as long as the modifications do not change the main idea of the movie, we would enhance the work of the original director by allowing the movie to be appreciated outside of its original cultural context.

If modern stories need to be modified this significantly to allow ancient audiences like Abraham to fully understand them, how much should the ancient stories of Abraham's day be modified so that they can be fully appreciated by modern audiences? Sometimes the changes should be significant, not because we want to distort God's Word; rather, we augment the stories of Scripture with dramatically appropriate historical and cultural information so that the original intent of their authors will be realized anew in our day. Our goal is to extend the ancient impact of these narratives to a contemporary audience.

The biblical stories were written under the inspiration of the Holy Spirit to have maximum impact on their original audience. They accomplished their task perfectly and cannot be improved upon. But the original recipients of these stories are long dead, and unless you are preaching to dead people, it is unwise to simply "rerun" these ancient narratives. To be faithful to the intent of the original writers of these stories, we need to add and reshape the material to communicate to the unique time and culture to which we minister. All preaching does this.

When you preach a "traditional" sermon from Galatians, you do not simply read the text ... in Koine Greek. In addition to translating the text to a language your congregation understands, you will probably add an introduction and conclusion. You will also outline "points" that are not found verbatim in the text. You may add some contemporary applications that Paul did not give to his original audience — perhaps even an illustration or two drawn from your own personal experience!

When you add this nontextual content to your sermons, are you playing fast and loose with the text? Are you being unfaithful? Of course not. Your goal in adding to the biblical text is simply to say to your congregation what Paul originally said to the Galatians. To add nontextual materials that help you extend Paul's purposes is not wrong. This is what all sermons do. It is what differentiates sermons from Scripture reading.

This is also what we must do with narrative sermons to preach them effectively. This is why the protagonist of your first-person sermon may or may not be the protagonist of the biblical story. What kind of protagonist should you have?

The first criteria in the selection of the main character for your sermon should be his or her proximity (physically and emotionally) to the action of the story, especially the unexpected twist of the story. One of the primary attributes of this sermon form is its ability to give a passionate eyewitness account of dramatic events. The more removed your main character is from the events of a story, the more emotionally distant your audience will be from the story. Hearing a former World Trade Tower office worker tell you how she managed to survive the terrorist attack of 9/11 is much more interesting than hearing the same information relayed by her second cousin once removed who was living in Sydney, Australia, at the time. When it comes to choosing a protagonist the first rule is: the closer the better. If at all possible, become the major character of a story.

When I preach Gideon's defeat of the Midianites in Judges 6 and 7, for example, I become Gideon. By taking on this character, I can give my audience unprecedented access to all the physical and emotional elements of this story. I can relate how unqualified I felt when the angel of the Lord asked me to save Israel out of Midian's hand. How terrified I was when God told me to send all but a mere three hundred men back home. And how elated I was to surprisingly triumph over the superior Midianite army. Gideon was present at all the key events, privy to all the information, and emotionally invested in the outcome of the story. For these reasons, Gideon is probably the best person to act as the protagonist in this narrative.

There are times, however, when you cannot be the major character. Sometimes you even have to invent a protagonist in order to tell the story. Why? Let me illustrate.

In 2 Kings 5 you have an emotional and action-packed story. This is wonderful material for a first-person sermon in which Naaman is the dominant character. He would be a fascinating character to portray! A highly successful commander in the army of the king of Aram, he found himself afflicted with leprosy. In his desperation to rid himself of this dread disease, Naaman takes the advice of an Israelite slave girl and travels to the king of Israel in search of a prophet who can cure him. The king then directs Naaman to Elisha's house.

Surprisingly, Elisha does not even come out to meet him! He simply sends a messenger with the instructions, "Go, wash yourself seven times in the Jordan, and your flesh will be restored and you will be cleansed" (2 Kings 5:10). As difficult as these instructions are for this proud commander, he obeys God's command. When he finishes dipping himself in the river the seventh time, he is cured! After trying in vain to give a gift of thanks to Elisha, Naaman heads home prepared to permanently worship the God of Israel. What a wonderful story!

So why not preach this narrative through the character of Naaman? He looks perfect! He can talk about how proud he was and how horrible it was to first discover he had leprosy. He can then go on to explain how humiliating it was to be asked to dip in the lousy Jordan River, and how ecstatic he was when he was cured! Why would you not want to be Naaman?

Why? Because Naaman was not present when the main event of the story, the unexpected twist, occurred. The story does not end when Naaman heads for home. In the scenes that follow, Gehazi pursues Naaman in order to personally profit from the commander's generosity. After telling a lie about an unexpected need that arose, Gehazi returns home laden with gifts. Elisha, armed with supernatural knowledge, confronts Gehazi about his disobedience. The story ends with a moment of dramatic irony. Gehazi is afflicted with the leprosy that Naaman once had. It jumped from the Gentile army officer to the Israelite servant of the prophet. Why? Because of the issue of obedience. It seems that God is colorblind. He does not care about our ethnic origins — just whether we are willing to respond to God with humble obedience. Naaman was obedient and was cured. Gehazi was disobedient and so was afflicted. What God looks for is humble obedience.

The reason I cannot tell this story through Naaman is that his character did not witness what happened to Gehazi. He missed the surprising twist of the story! I could have chosen to be Gehazi, to speak the story. At least he was present at the surprising twist, but he would have missed all the early events of Naaman's life. In order to preach this story as a first person, I need to personify a character who was present at the beginning as well as the end of the narrative. But who? There isn't a character in the biblical narrative who meets this criterion in the biblical story. I have to create a new character.

When I preached this narrative, the character I created was Naaman's armor bearer. Such a character seemed plausible for a number of reasons. A military official of Naaman's stature is likely to have had one. An armor bearer was a highly trusted confidant who would have accompanied Naaman during all his military campaigns and would have been familiar with his private life. Since the prestige of an armor bearer would have been linked to that of his commander, he would travel the same emotional journey as Naaman throughout the story.

But how could the armor bearer be present at the unexpected twist? If you look at the biblical text, you will see that Naaman gave Gehazi a sizeable gift — a gift so significant, in fact, that it seems unlikely that the servant of the prophet could have carried it back home unaided. In my first-person sermon, I had Naaman offer the services of his trusted armor bearer to help Gehazi get home safely — and witness the confrontation with Elisha and Gehazi's leprous fate. As the armor bearer hurries to catch up with Naaman at the end of the story, he reflects on the lesson he has learned: "The God of Israel is not like any other god I have ever heard of. Not only is he all-powerful, but he values humble obedience above everything else!"

You should wisely select or create the protagonist who has the potential to most clearly communicate the big idea of the narrative. Above all else, you want an unambiguous presentation of biblical truth.

Caution!

- If you find yourself creating characters regularly, be careful not to keep creating similar characters. I have a tendency to make all of my created characters look as if they are walking off the pages of a Horatio Alger novel — poor kids from the wrong side of the track who made good. Wherever possible, use one of the characters in the biblical narrative. This will help ensure that you are working with characters that are believable, credible, and varied. If you can't, be creative. Don't let yourself get stuck in a repetitive rut.

- Sometimes you can speak the message of a passage in a fresh way by relating it through the life of an antagonist. For example, you could tell the story of Christ's resurrection from the perspective of the Roman commander in John 18 who came with a detachment of soldiers to arrest Jesus. "I was under orders to control this situation . . . but who can control a man like this? I am a seasoned competent military professional, but no one could control the events of this week, because no one can control Jesus. He is obviously more than just a man. He is God. And he is beyond my jurisdiction."[3]

- Make sure that the protagonist will adequately reflect the emotion of the narrative. Good Friday should end down. Easter and Christmas should shoot for the moon! Make sure that you select protagonists who can naturally reflect the mood of the text as well as its meaning.

- Preach first-person sermons at Christmas and Easter. By communicating these well-known stories through the eyes of a different character every year, you will ensure that your congregation hears these old, old stories in fresh, new ways.

- Do not select an inappropriate character. Do not portray a character of the opposite sex (no cross-dressing allowed). Do not be an animal. (I don't want to hear of anyone being the donkey that carried Mary to Bethlehem!) Do not be an inanimate object. (Don't be one of the rocks that Abraham used to build an altar to sacrifice Isaac.) Choices such as these can devalue the pulpit as well as our ministry.

Once you have selected the best possible protagonist, you must give him or her a *dominant, defining characteristic*. This characteristic may be your character's primary asset or tragic flaw, but it will always be determined by the exegesis you have done on the biblical text. This defining characteristic may be selfish ambition (Judas), a love for family that exceeds even love for God (Eli), or the simple, unadulterated love of a father for his daughter (Jairus), but the central characteristic must be present and reflect the original narrative.

This defining attribute is the spine of your character. It gives your character coherence by explaining why they make the choices they do. It makes sense out of the story. After you have identified your protagonist and have recognized their defining attribute, you can begin to develop and enrich his or her personality.

It is important that you invest the time and energy to develop your protagonist significantly. This will be crucial when you get ready to deliver your first-person sermon. In the development of your main character you will begin to see your protagonist as more than just a disembodied attribute or a walking theological lesson. Your goal is to get to know the protagonist as well as his mother, spouse, and best friend knew him. You must see this character as a real flesh-and-blood person at ease in the home environment. Do not skip the work that this requires. It is critical to effective first-person sermons because it is here that the main character in your message takes shape and becomes genuine. If he or she never becomes real to you, this person will never become real to those who hear your message. You will preach a plastic sermon.

Here are the factors to keep in mind to guide your character development.

- Background
  - ✍ Discover where your character grew up and where they live during the story. Does their place of origin have any bearing on the story? Are they more comfortable in the city or the country? What were their formative childhood influences?
  - ✍ What are their primary skills? How did they acquire those abilities? How do they employ them?
  - ✍ What is their social station? Are they upper- or lower-class people? Rich or poor? How does their socioeconomic status influence their life or differentiate them from their neighbors? How much formal and informal education do they have?
  - ✍ What is their family makeup? Did either parent die? Were they close to their parents and family? Were they raised at home? If not, why not?
  - ✍ Have they faced significant disappointments in life? How did this shape them?
- Physical characteristics
  - ✍ How would you describe their race, age, physical strength, carriage, overall health, dress, and speech? Are they physically unique in any way or do they suffer from any physical maladies or defects? Are they particularly good looking?

- Mental characteristics
  - ✍ What is their native intelligence? Do they learn easily? Are they particularly creative or innovative?
- Emotional characteristics
  - ✍ What adjectives best describe the protagonist's temperament? Impetuous? Cautious? Determined? Hot-headed? Temperate? Passionate?
  - ✍ Do they have capacity for deep feeling?
  - ✍ Do they cope with change or are they easily overwhelmed?
- Spiritual/moral characteristics
  - ✍ Where are they on their spiritual journey? How would you characterize their relationship with God? Are they lovers, strangers, or something in between?
  - ✍ Do they start out the story as spiritual leaders in their community? Do their peers regard them as such by the end the story?
  - ✍ Is your protagonist willing to cut ethical corners? Why or why not?
  - ✍ What makes them angry?
  - ✍ What would cause them to throw a party?

Out of all the work you have just done to understand your protagonist, take the time to identify the most significant attributes.

- Vital traits
  - ✍ Take out a blank piece of paper and write your protagonist's name at the top of the list. Of all the traits that you have identified, list the top five on the left side of the page. On the opposite side of the page write why these traits are so important. Explain why the story cannot be told without these attributes.

Understanding your protagonist is a significant task. It requires you to think deeply, research widely, and invest a significant amount of time. It can also be discouraging when you know that at the end of the process you will probably have more information on this character than you can possibly use in one sermon. That is OK. There are two reasons why, when it comes to data about your protagonist, "the more the merrier."

First, like an expert portrait artist, you must have more paint available than you need to create a likeness of your subject. Good artists have an abundance of colors on their palette as they sit down to work. But they don't throw all of the paint at their disposal on the canvas. Instead, they selectively apply only the most appropriate colors on select locations of the canvas. I have never known an artist who was particularly concerned if at the conclusion of the project, he or she had paint left over. The goal of artists is not to use up paint. Rather, their goal is to use the paint at their disposal as effectively as possible to create the most lifelike representation of their subject possible. They want their painting to perfectly portray their subject. That is our goal as well. When we begin writing our first-person sermon, we want to be able to start with a palette laden with all available colors.

A second reason for doing extensive character development work on your protagonist is the character insight that it provides. The more details you are able to gather, the deeper you will be able to gaze into the heart of your main character. You will discover what makes him or her "tick." A holistic understanding of your protagonist enables their motivations to come into focus. Understanding motivation is critical in the development of a credible protagonist.

Your listeners need to understand why the protagonist was willing to undertake the difficult journey outlined in the biblical narrative. What is it that propels your protagonist on toward their goal despite the increasing opposition and suffering that they are experiencing? Why are they willing to endure this pain? Why is their objective so important to them? What need will it satisfy?

Your answers to these questions will reveal your protagonist's core convictions. As the base motivation of your protagonist begins to rise to the surface of your consciousness, be sure to write it down. Writing clarifies thought, and you need to be clear about your protagonist's motivation. When you are sure you understand that base motivation, take an additional step by asking yourself: "Will my audience relate to this character?"

Personal Identification

Stories told by strangers can be interesting, but true stories told by the people we care about are riveting. Compelling narrative sermons feature a protagonist that the audience genuinely cares about. Congregations listen carefully to stories that feature a protagonist with whom they have formed an emotional bond.

Bonding is easiest when the listeners like the protagonist. We make friends with people who are similar to us. We make friends with people who share our values and priorities. When we cry and cheer, we do so for similar reasons. If your protagonist is the kind of person that your listeners would like to have over for dinner, it should be relatively easy for you to help them emotionally connect. As powerful as likeability may be, however, it is not the most essential component of emotional bonding. It is possible to care about people we would not want as friends.

The most important critical component of emotional bonding is *identification*. As dissimilar as your listeners may be from your protagonist, your audience needs to see some part of themselves in the protagonist. At some level, your listeners need to sense a kinship even if there are few superficial similarities. Thirty-year-old parents of two are quite capable of bonding with single, eighty-year-old widowers. What identification requires is character resemblance. Listeners need to resonate with the core motivation of your protagonist. While they may not approve of what your protagonist did, they must say, "I know what that feels like! I could imagine responding to that situation in a similar way." This is not as hard to accomplish as you might think, for there is no sin that exceeds the human capacity for rationalization.

- A bank robber may try to justify his actions by explaining that he lost his benefits when his job was outsourced overseas and his wife needed expensive cancer medication. We may not agree with his theft, but we know how desperate we would become if that happened to us. "Desperate times lead to desperate measures," says the bank robber. We can put ourselves in his shoes — feel his pain — even if we would not do what he did.
- A woman has a brief affair after discovering her husband's longtime sexual indiscretions. We don't condone her sin, but we understand how desperately injured she must have been by this discovery and how in the disorientation of her pain she lashed out at her husband the way he had hurt her. Her actions are sinful. We do not condone them. But we can understand why she would do such a thing. Part of us resonates with her motivation. We sympathize with her.

Take your listeners beyond the protagonist's actions and help them empathize with the motivation behind the behavior. You must help them understand, not condone, the protagonist's reasons. To help others emotionally connect with a protagonist, you need to enter into the emotional life of your protagonist.

If you are to fully comprehend your character, you will need to find points of contact between yourself and your protagonist. How are you similar to your character? Can you remember when you faced a similar situation and made a similar choice? Rummage through the forgotten closets of your life looking for occasions similar to those experienced by your character. If you are honest and self-aware, you will soon discover in your life, even if only in seed form, the same vices and virtues that bloom in the life of your protagonist. Let's use Samson as an illustration.

On the pages of the book of Judges, we discover that Samson was a very earthy man. In spite of the clear command of God, he chose to disobey his Nazirite vows in favor of sensual pursuits. When he broke the final vow, he lost his amazing strength and the ability to do what God had called him to do: deliver Israel from the Philistines. Samson's decision to sin reduced his ministry effectiveness.

If you are going to preach this narrative effectively, you will have to personally identify with him. Even if you have not destroyed your ministry with willful sin (may this never happen!), I am sure there have been times in your life when the lure of sin was so strong that the kingdom consequences of your actions began to dim. Perhaps a moment when a parishioner made herself sexually available. Or during a season of personal financial pressure you stumbled on a quantity of cash left out in the church office and available for theft. Were you tempted even for a moment? What if you had surrendered to that temptation? What could have been the consequences of that sin? How might your ministry have been affected? If God's enemies had then held up you and your sin for public ridicule, as they did with Samson, how would you have felt? To disgrace the God who chose you for great things? To let God's people down? And for what? A momentary point of pleasure. Was that pleasure worth the pain? Of course not! If you could turn back time, you would do it in a heartbeat. But what is done is done.

The seed of the sin that led to tragedy in Samson's life lives in my heart. We are alike in kind if not degree. By personally identifying with my protagonist, I am able to help my people form an emotional bond as well. They begin to care about Samson, and they intuitively learn that the lesson of Samson's life applies to them. Emotional interlock is an important part of effective narrative preaching.

STEP FOUR | Create your antagonist.

If the protagonist's story is going to capture the imagination of your audience, he or she needs to face significant obstacles. These obstacles usually are personified in one individual: the antagonist. Antagonists directly oppose the protagonist's goals. Their goal is to stop the protagonist and — if the story is interesting — make it look until the very end of the story as if they will succeed.

A good antagonist is an important element of a good story. What makes an antagonist effective?

- *Effective antagonists are more powerful than the protagonist.* Saul has far more resources than David does. Goliath outweighs David. Moses seems bush league when he asks Pharaoh to let Israel go. If the protagonist were more powerful, there would be no story. The protagonist would simply swat the antagonist aside as he strode toward his easy objective. Worthy protagonists need — and deserve — worthy antagonists. The opposition of the antagonist allows the main character to stretch, grow, and accomplish a meaningful victory. Protagonists can only be as compelling as the force of the antagonist allows them to be.
- *Effective antagonists are people.* They are more than just blind irrational agents of hate and anger. They have discernable and rational objectives and motivations. A good example of an effective contemporary antagonist is Darth Vader. Throughout the *Star Wars* movies, Darth Vader is unquestionably evil. We discover, however, that Darth was not always evil. He started out as a gifted young man with a good

heart. It was only after his mother was murdered and he was the victim of a series of perceived personal injustices that he became so evil. The audience realizes that the source of Darth Vader's evil actions is his childhood pain. Adults are inhabited by the children they used to be. Good storytellers recognize and harness this as they develop their antagonists as well as their protagonists.

- *Effective antagonists are designed for their protagonists.* The strengths of the bad guy are the weaknesses of the good guy, and vice versa. You can see this displayed in the interaction between David and Saul.

Shylock

One of the best antagonists ever developed was Shylock in Shakespeare's *Merchant of Venice*. He was the money-lender who proposed to exact a pound of living flesh for an unpaid bill. He was unquestionably evil! However, Shakespeare realized that he also had to make him human. To accomplish this Shakespeare revealed a series of injustices that made Shylock so vindictive, and then gave him a soliloquy to express his angst:

Hath not a Jew eyes?
If you prick us, do we not bleed?
If you poison us, do we not die?
And if you wrong us, shall we not
   revenge?

Merchant of Venice, Act 3, Scene 1

As much as we may dislike Shylock, we cannot help feeling some sympathy for him. Good antagonists are three-dimensional. They have emotions and feelings. Don't make them too bad to be true.

David and Saul:

In 1 Samuel 23, Saul, the antagonist is using all the power at his disposal to hunt down and kill David. In 1 Samuel 24, however, the reader witnesses David, the protagonist, refusing to kill defenseless Saul while he relieves himself at the back of a cave.

Likewise, throughout 1 Samuel, Saul is obsessed with eliminating all rivals for his throne — especially David. How interesting to read in 2 Samuel 9, therefore, that David asks, "Is there anyone still left of the house of Saul to whom I can show kindness for Jonathan's sake?" David shows himself to be as kind and generous as Saul was cruel and selfish. The biblical narrator did an exceptional job in matching Saul and David as antagonist and protagonist. The strengths of the antagonists are the weaknesses of the protagonist.

It is never easy giving birth, but when the pain is over, every mother I have ever met has said that the joy of bringing her baby into the world was worth it. You will say the same thing. If you endure through the painful process of creating authentic protagonists and antagonists, you will have birthed wonderful characters capable of meaningfully communicating the big idea of your narrative passage. Your babies will touch lives with the Word of God. Don't shrink from the pain of bringing them into the world. Anticipate the blessing.

NOTES FOR CHAPTER FIVE

1. When a first-person sermon is not appropriate, you may consider some of the additional homiletical options outlined in chapter 8.
2. Robert Mckee, *Story* (New York: Regan, 1997), 115.
3. With thanks to Shawn Wicks.

Chapter Six

COMPLETING THE HOMILETICAL TASK

I have long been fascinated by animation. I marvel as I watch Disney artists not only put pen to paper and create characters, but then, with the power of their pens, bring those characters to life. Snow White becomes more than just a drawing. She becomes a graceful lady who sings like a bird and embarks on wondrous adventures. Your pen has the same power as the Disney animators. Now that you have created your characters, give them a home and set them off on a grand journey of faith that displays the big idea of your biblical text.

 Set the story.

How well do you know the neighborhood where you grew up? Pretty well, I'm sure. You know the shortcuts — where and when it is safe and where you shouldn't go after dark. You know where to go to find sin and how best to avoid it. You know which dogs bark and which stairs creak. You know its history as well as the emotional significance of its landmarks. You know your hometown. It feels as comfortable as a pair of old jeans. It is your home.

You need to be just as familiar with the home of your protagonists. When you tell their stories, you are taking over their lives. You begin to live on their turf. Your goal is to know it as well as they do. You can't drive into town with a tourist map, ask a few questions at the information booth, and pretend that you know the town as well as someone who grew up there.

To tell the biblical story well, you must know where the story is situated. If you don't, you will default back to the mental images created in your Sunday school days. The town will look like the photographs in the back of a children's Bible, and your story will slide into a cliché. When first-person sermons seem trite, it is because the preacher does not adequately understand the setting of the story. Narrative clichés can be traced to a single source: The writer does not know the world of his story.

Period, Duration, and Location

Period is a story's place in time. It is knowing what was going on in the world at the time of the narrative. You understand your story's period when you know what the headlines were in the local newspaper. What the people gossiped about at lunchtime. What frightened their children at bedtime. Period also includes the manners and customs of this period. How did the people of that time eat? Get married and divorced?

Duration is the length of time that the story spans within the lives of your characters. Does the story take decades to happen? Years? Months? Days? Hours?

Location is the story's physical dimension. What is the story's specific geography? What did it look like? Was it flat desert or mountainous high country? Do the physical characteristics of the land influence the story? Were there bandits hiding in the area or was it physically safe? How far apart are the places mentioned in the narrative? In what town did the story take place? On what streets? In what building? In what room?

I recommend that you find photographs of where the story takes place. I have long used and recommended pictorial encyclopedias and dictionaries. Atlases and archaeological reference works that feature drawings and photographs help as well. When you see where your story takes place, you will be able to describe it to others. If it is real to you, it will be real to your audience.

Resources that give you insight into the culture and practices of your story are worth their weight in platinum. When you find them, buy them. I have the following resources particularly useful:

J. D. Douglas. *The Illustrated Bible Dictionary.* 3 volumes. Leicester: Inter-Varsity Press, 1998.

Roland De Vaux. *Ancient Israel: Its Life and Institutions.* Grand Rapids: Eerdmans, 1997.

Philip J. King and Lawrence E. Stager. *Life in Biblical Israel.* Louisville: Westminster John Knox, 2001.

Merrill C. Tenney. *The Zondervan Encyclopedia of the Bible.* 5 volumes. Grand Rapids: Zondervan, 1977.

J. A. Thompson. *Handbook of Life in Bible Times.* Downers Grove, Ill.: InterVarsity Press, 1986.

After this hard research is over, however, I recommend that you utilize some sanctified imagination. Using the hard data you have collected, lean back and ask yourself: "What would it be like to live in my character's life hour by hour, day by day?" Take out some paper and, in vivid detail, sketch out how you think that your character would have lived his or her life — that is, worked, shopped, traveled, recreated, worshiped, and so on. Use your creativity to fuse the various components of your research into a coherent picture of your character. A good imagination is a critical component of good biblical interpretation and communication.

STEP SIX | Plot the action.

Stories are ideas wrapped up in life, concepts dressed in humanity. They express their meaning through the action and in the burning emotion of the dramatic climax. They are a creative demonstration of truth, the living proof of an idea.

As you plan your story, begin by placing your idea at the climax. Draw a large circle on a blank piece of paper. This is your mono-mythic cycle. At the very bottom of the circle, make a mark representing the climax of your story. This is your goal. It is the surprising twist in the plot — the moment of aha! It is where the complement of your subject can be seen. This is the moment when the big idea of the narrative is finally revealed.

The purpose of the plot is to magnify the idea contained in the climax. A good plot helps the idea explode in the mind and heart of the listeners. It demands that we give it a hearing. It insists that we notice and consider it. A good plot crowns the idea king. It ensures that everything is subservient to the central concept. Whatever draws the listener's attention toward the idea is utilized. Whatever does not contribute to the communication of the idea is eliminated — scraped off the plot like a barnacle from the bottom of a boat. If you have not done so already, write down the big idea of your story on a post-it note and stick it to the corner of your computer monitor. This will help you keep interesting irrelevancies from creeping into your sermon.

Take a look at the scenes that the biblical narrator originally used to communicate the idea.

- What cultural information would the original audience have had that you will need to provide to your listeners? How will you communicate this additional information?
- Will you need to introduce new characters or expand the role of any existing characters?
- How much back-story does your contemporary audience need to put this ancient story into proper context?
- Do you need to rearrange the order of the scenes?
- Should you compress a number of existing scenes into a single scene?
- Are additional scenes required?
- How much time will be available for you to preach this sermon?

Once you have asked and answered these questions, mark out and title the scenes in the order that they will appear in your sermon on the left (fall) side of the mono-mythic cycle. When this is done, take out the Scene Development Chart included at the back of this book (appendix 2) and use it to detail the various scenes you will be using when you preach your sermon.

Be sure to detail the dramatic purpose of each of your scenes. This is critical. A first-person sermon is not a lecture. It is the dramatic historical presentation of a biblical idea. If your sermon does not have drama, you don't have a first-person sermon, just a bad lecture. How can you increase the dramatic power of your sermon? Increase the conflict. Drama is conflict. Conflict is drama.

Increase Conflict and Tension

As countless engaged couples have learned through the years, diamonds are best appreciated when laid on black velvet. Only when we examine these jewels against a jet-black background are we able to appreciate their sparkling beauty. If the jeweler were to place the same diamond on a background of beige corduroy, you could not fully recognize the magnificence of the jewel.

Strong conflict does for narratives what black velvet does for diamonds. Conflict allows us to see and appreciate the full magnificence of the big idea of a biblical narrative. Without a background of conflict, a big idea can seem weak and insipid. If you want your audience to gasp in wonderment when they see the idea God placed in a biblical passage, then display it on the darkest background possible. Increase the tension and conflict in your sermon to the maximum. You can never have too much tension and conflict in a first-person sermon.

A good way to begin increasing the tension of your sermon is by stating your big idea in the reverse. Do to your idea what a negative does to a photograph. Show the same image in the reverse. Let me illustrate. We saw in chapter 4 that the exegetical idea of Daniel 1 was as follows:

Subject: What happened when Daniel and his friends refused to defile themselves by consuming the royal food and wine?

Complement: God gave them better health and academic success than all of the students who ate the defiling food.

What would the opposite — the negative — of this idea be?

Anti-subject: Why shouldn't Daniel and his friends go ahead and eat the royal food and wine?

Anti-complement: Not only does the food taste good, it will also keep them on their positive career track.

When you state the negative of the biblical idea, you hear the temptations that Satan whispers into our ear. You hear lies from the pit of hell. You hear the seductive lines that the enemy of our souls uses to shipwreck our souls. Conflict occurs in your sermon when you use Satan's playbook to try to destroy your protagonist:

Come on Daniel, what's the bid deal? Who cares about a little meat? Doesn't it smell good? Everybody else is eating it. Are you sure that God would want you to throw your career away over such a small issue? I agree with your principles, Daniel, but wouldn't it be wiser for you to wait until you get your career safely underway before making such a scene? Think how embarrassed you will be when you wash out of the training program and are sent home in disgrace.

You need to develop the skill of looking at a biblical idea as a cynic. Do you remember the old TV show *M.A.S.H.*? Imagine Father Mulcahy standing in a tent in Korea preaching the legitimate big idea of the biblical text. Just as he is hitting stride, however, Captain "Hawkeye" Pierce staggers into the back of the tent, a glass of homemade hooch in hand, and begins to listen to the sermon. How do you think this irreverent skeptic would respond to the biblical idea being espoused by Father Mulcahy? How would he critique it? How would he mock and ridicule it?

You need to create such a withering attack against your protagonist that your audience genuinely fears that he or she will not stand! The psychological possibility of failure becomes possible. It has to. If we think that a happy ending is inevitable, there is no point watching. If you have no conflict, you have no tension. If you have no tension, you have no interest. If your listeners are not interested, your sermon is finished — even if you keep on talking.

When you subject the big idea of your narrative to the scathing disbelief personified by Hawkeye Pierce, you are generating the real-world objections, skepticism, and criticism you need to create a compelling first-person sermon. This is what you need to increase the conflict and tension in your story. It darkens the background of your story and helps your listeners appreciate the magnificent beauty of its big idea. It also increases the likelihood that the sermon will result in significant life changes for your listeners.

When it comes to tension, narrative sermons resemble bows and arrows. Increasing tension in a first-person sermon by adding conflict has the same effect as increasing tension on a bow by pulling back on the string. An arrow released under pressure by a bow hunter will strike its target with deadly force. A big idea released under pressure by a first-person preacher will also make a significant impact on its target audience. The greater the tension, the greater the impact.

If you want your sermon to make a difference, increase its tension. As you work for tension, however, be aware of the two most common tension-deadening mistakes that preachers commonly make.

Common Mistakes

One common tension-deadening mistake of first-person preachers is beginning the sermon by communicating a huge amount of biblical or cultural data.

It is not unusual for preachers to spend the first five minutes of their sermon wandering around in their research material. This is deadly. The essence of a story is action. You want your idea to come alive, not be discussed. Something needs to happen soon.

Think of how long it takes for the action to begin in a James Bond or Arnold Schwarzenegger movie. While you may not be writing the screenplay for an action flick, the principle of starting your dramatic sermon with movement is valid. As you look at your mono-mythic plot structure, identify the *inciting event* of your story and place it close to the beginning of your sermon.

The inciting event is the reason why your protagonist was spurred into action. What was it that caused your character to decide to act today? The discontent that they felt about their situation had probably been simmering for some time. What caused it to suddenly reach the boiling point? What was it that got them off the couch? This inciting event will have succeeded in motivating your character because you have touched a core psychological need of your protagonist. That need is the subject of your sermon — the first half of your sermon's idea. It asks the question that your sermon will answer. Let me illustrate.

In Daniel 1, the story opens with our hero ecstatic about his good fortune. He is seated in an opulent banquet hall while being serenaded by some of the world's finest musicians. Around him are some of the best and the brightest young people ever to walk the earth, selected for these prestigious seats because of their outstanding attributes and qualifications. They are the best of the best. And they are anticipating the best of all possible futures: prosperous careers with the most secure and successful government that the world has ever seen. This is good!

Suddenly the volume of the music increases and the tune changes to the national anthem. Chefs file in single file from a door on the left of the hall holding on silver platters the most appealing food Daniel has ever seen. A lot better than what was available in burned-out Jerusalem! The aroma was irresistible. As the chefs brought their creations to the tables, a Babylonian priest stood up: "Servants of the gods, let us rejoice in the bounty that they have bestowed upon us. This food comes to you from the temple. It has just been offered to the great god Marduk and, in a display grace, he offers it to you. Let us all eat with thanksgiving!"

This is the inciting event! The crisis that forced godly Daniel to action. And it raises the question of the sermon: What will happen when God's people refuse to allow their culture to pressure them into sin? The subject of the passage has been raised. Now we need to ratchet up the conflict and tension of the story to a fever pitch. I want everyone on the edge of their seat as they wonder about the fate of these godly boys. I want them to begin to personally identify with these young men. I want the lives of my listeners to begin to intertwine with the lives of the biblical characters.

The second tension-deadening mistake of first-person preachers is the soliloquy. I am amazed how often we preachers want our protagonists to stand up and give an extended discourse in which they display their theological insights on life. These soliloquies are to dramatic sermons what a wet quilt is to a campfire. They put the fire out by suffocating the life out of it. Epistles talk about theology in abstract terms. Narrative literature displays theology in everyday life. Paul explains it in Romans. Abraham lives it in Genesis.

Your first-person sermon should show us the truth, not engage in extensive discussion about it. Yes, Shakespeare was able to use soliloquy for dramatic effect. But he was perhaps the greatest writer outside of Scripture. We are not. Avoid long speeches.

Stop the Story

Conflict is interesting. Tension causes us to lean forward in our seats. We want our airport novel to keep us wondering "who done it" until the very last page. Then we want it to end. When the tension is gone from a story, the interest of the audience will quickly dissipate.

Expert storytellers will not reveal the unexpected twist of their stories until the very last moment. This enables them to wring the maximum amount of tension out of the plot. Once they finally do reveal the unexpected twist of the plot, they stop the story as quickly as possible. When the climax of a story is reached, the big idea of the narrative has been revealed. The secret is out. The punch line has been delivered. The tension is gone. You have only a few moments left to bring your story back up the mono-mythic cycle to summer. If you keep going (especially if you start outlining "points" from the passage!), you will be ruining a good thing. Quit when you are done.

How to Tell If Your Proposed Plot Is an Effective Vehicle

You have now sketched out the basic plot on your mono-mythic cycle, and your Scene Development Sheets are beginning to fill up. Before you go to all the work of manuscripting, however, it would be helpful to know if you are on the right track. Is there a way to know in advance if your proposed plot is an effective vehicle for the big idea of your text? Yes. There are three.

1. Double Check

The first way to test the integrity of your plot structure is to compare it with the biblical text. Compare your Scene Analysis charts with your Scene Development sheets. How similar are they? If the plot you are planning to preach is identical to the plot used by the biblical writer, you can be fairly sure that you need to do some more work on your plot. Only on very rare occasions should you simply "rerun the story." Almost always it should be modified.

Remember, while you are communicating the same idea as the biblical author, you are speaking to a much different audience. Look at the difference that just one generation can make. If today's Baby Boomers are significantly different from Generation X and Generation Y, think about how great the gulf is between the biblical audiences and ours. You wouldn't just read ancient letters to your listeners (like the book of Galatians) and expect them to fully comprehend it. Why would you just tell ancient stories and expect understanding?

2. Climax

A second test you can apply to your plot structure is that of climax. Is the climax in your story exactly the same as the biblical text? If not, you have a serious problem. The unexpected twist in your story releases the tension of the story and reveals the complement of the narrative. If you have a different twist to your story, you are preaching a different idea than the biblical story. You may have a great story, but it is not the biblical story. Your sermon is not expository — it is not exposing the idea that the original author embedded into the original passage. Good sermon, wrong text.

3. Character Arc

The final test you can apply to your plot is that of character arc. As you look over the structure of your proposed story, does your protagonist undergo some significant change? Does he or she develop and grow? They need to. True character is revealed by pressure. Who people seem to be is probably not who they really are. A hidden nature waits concealed behind a façade of traits. The only way we can ever get to know a character in depth is by seeing the choices that they make under pressure. We expect extreme pressure to show us something about the character we had not seen before.

If the sermon begins with a "good father" and by the end of the sermon all we have is a "good father" — with no secrets, hidden passions, or significant growth — your listeners will be disappointed. Repetitious and predictable behavior is not wrong. Shallow, nondimensional people do exist. But they are boring. Good stories have interesting characters. They display how the protagonist was shaped by the events of the narrative to become

"Can we just cut to the moral tonight?"

Copyright 2004. Reprinted with the permission of Mike Twohy and the Washington Post Writers Group. All rights reserved.

more than he or she was before it began. In so doing, they point the way for our own personal development.

It takes a lot more effort to develop a captivating story. But when you see people cut to the heart with the Word of God, it is worth it. You will never want to shortcut the sermon writing process again!

STEP SEVEN | Determine the perspective.

Before you start writing your manuscript, you need to determine where the storyteller will be standing as they tell this story. I am not referring here to their physical location on the platform. I am talking about the perspective from which they will tell the story. There are three legitimate perspective options for you to consider. Pick the one that you think will best communicate the idea of your passage.

Perspective Option 1

Your storyteller can invite the audience to go back in their imagination to the ancient life and time of the original events.

> Welcome! Welcome! Don't be bashful, come closer and gather around the fire. It is cold out there in the dark.
>
> *(Turning around he shouts)* Sarah! Sarah! We have guests! Please bring some food for our newfound friends. They have obviously traveled a long way.

Here the audience is being indirectly informed that they have been transported back to the time and place of Abraham. Characters speaking from this perspective must strictly limit their knowledge to the ancient world. They cannot make any direct or implied reference to contemporary culture. You must operate according to the rules you have established. The advantage of this position is that the audience will come to really experience the biblical world. The ancient will become contemporary.

Perspective Option 2

The storyteller can emerge into the present from the past to speak to a contemporary audience.

> I am sorry to be so nervous this morning. I am not used to speaking to groups of people like this. Back when I lived, I was neither a rabbi nor a prophet. I was a carpenter. I worked with wood, not words.

Here Joseph, the father of Jesus, walks into our world. This perspective allows the storyteller to have a very limited awareness of our modern world.

Their contemporary knowledge is restricted to what an ancient could comprehend if they were "beamed" directly into your sanctuary to speak their message. You have a slight amount of latitude here to make contemporary references, but do not abuse this. If you do, you will destroy the integrity of the sermonic genre and render your sermon either incomprehensible or ridiculous — or both.

Perspective Option 3

Your character can involve the audience as current participants in the historical past. Consider the following introduction to a message on Daniel 4.

> I was going to begin by thanking you noble people for joining me at my palace today. However, such a welcome would not have been appropriate. After all, what choice did you have? When I, King Nebuchadnezzar speak, everyone obeys. There is no one who thwarts my will. I am the greatest ruler of our age, indeed of all ages! I am sorry for that. Forgive me.
>
> My pride has often got the best of me in the past. It almost destroyed me. Until the God of the Hebrews, the one true God, taught me a lesson that I will never forget, one that I know he would want you to know as well. I summoned you all here today so that you as leaders of people could learn the lesson that I learned.

Here you are recreating the actual time in the past when the events of the story took place. This can be a powerful type of storytelling because it allows the main character to talk directly to the listeners and treat them as part of the story. Obviously, the character can only refer to the ancient world. You must do the same.

 Create your lesser characters.

Now you can resurrect or invent the characters you need to advance the plot or shine light on your significant characters. As a rule of thumb, the fewer the characters you add, the better. Even though you will intentionally keep these people two-dimensional (they are only functionaries), you do not want to overly complicate your story. Keep your first-person sermon as straightforward and uncomplicated as possible. Simplicity is a virtue.

 Write the manuscript.

Now you are finally ready to start writing your first-person sermon. At this point in the sermon preparation process, it is easy to fall into despair. "Look how much work it has taken so far and I have not even begun writing! How much longer is this going to take?"

Take heart, however. If you have followed the steps I have laid out, you are closer to the finish line than you think. (And if you skipped some, you are further away than you realize.) By this time you know the story and the characters so well and have the big idea so firmly affixed in your mind that the story is likely to just flow out of you. After doing all the background work, my biggest problem is trying to type fast enough. The words, images, and dialogue avalanche out of the text.

Start with the unexpected twist in your story. This is your destination. You will find that it is easier to tailor the rest of your sermon to this one critical point if you know precisely where it is going. As you write out this dramatic moment, do two things. First, show the idea in action. Make sure that we see the big idea of the text acted out by the characters. Make the idea of the story as dramatically plain and obvious as you possibly can. Second, however, I recommend that you also state the big idea of the text directly. Supplement the visual with the audio.

I realize that narrative purists disagree with me on this issue. They insist that if you tell a story with sufficient skill, the audience will easily spot the central idea of the story rising out of the actions of the various characters. I am used to being criticized on this issue.

But I also know how frequently and easily communication can break down. Even when we are talking to those who love and understand us, it is not uncommon for our words to be misunderstood. There are many occasions when, although we have done our very best to be clear, misunderstandings creep into our conversations. You are not understood as often as you think you are. As much as I want my conversations to be clear, I cannot afford to have my sermon misunderstood. The stakes are far too high! I would rather be redundant than obscure.

For this reason I speak the preaching idea of my text as forcefully and clearly as I possibly can. I don't want anyone to leave without hearing what God wanted them to hear. Write out sentences in advance. Don't leave it to chance. The stakes are too high. Be as clear as possible. Be as memorable as you can.

Once you have written out how you want the sermon to end, go back to the beginning and write out the entire sermon starting from the inciting event.

- As your fingers fly, *keep in mind that you are not writing an essay.* Write as if you were talking. This is more like a TV script than a Billy Graham sermon.
- *Bring your character to life.* Climb into your character's skin (this is possible after all the work that you have done) and write what you see as you look out of their eyes. Let us see them sweat in the heat. Struggle in the midst of the conflict and descend into despair when all seems lost. Your goal is to make the story authentic. Real. Think through your story with all of your senses. Connect with your audi-

ence's sense of smell, taste, sight, hearing, and touch in your manuscript. Use more verbs than adjectives.

- *Slow down the time* to give emphasis to those parts of the story that you do not want your listeners to miss. You will probably want to be in slow motion by the time you get to the twist in the plot. Time is elastic. Stretch it to suit your purposes.

- *Humor can help you.* While this is not an excuse for frustrated stand-up comics to strut their stuff, do not make the mistake of setting it entirely aside. Humor is an enormously powerful dramatic and persuasive tool. What we laugh at we agree with. As you construct your message, feel free to use your listener's funny bone to bond your listeners with the characters and ideas of your passage. If, however, your narrative passage does not lend itself to humor if humor is not compatible with your personality, do not force it. I would rather watch a schoolteacher scrape his or her fingernails across a blackboard than watch someone try to be funny. Humor is a tool not a necessity.

- *Emotion is critical.* You need to help your listeners weep with those who are weeping in your sermon. We need to despair with those who have given up hope. And we need to fall in love along with the newlyweds. Effective delivery can help generate the emotion that you are looking for, but it starts with your manuscript. Structure your story to touch hearts as well as heads.

STEP TEN | Decide about props.

As you write your manuscript, you may find yourself wanting to use a physical object to help you tell your story. This is a legitimate dramatic option. Occasionally an item can embody the big idea of your sermon. It is gradually transformed into an object lesson as you preach your sermon. While this may not happen frequently, when it is appropriate it can be an effective dramatic instrument.

When I preached Jacob, for example, I walked up to the platform leaning heavily on a wooden walking stick. At the end of the sermon, I held up my stick in triumph. It was a reminder of the day that I had wrestled with God!

STEP ELEVEN | Refine your manuscript.

The most efficient way to get your manuscript from first draft to finished edition is to say it aloud. Find a room where you know you will not be disturbed and read it aloud as you walk around. Don't sit down to read. You are far more likely to treat your manuscript as an essay if you are seated. It's not. It is much more like a conversation, so stand up and, holding your papers in one hand, read it aloud. As you do, make sure your voice is as expressive and forceful as it will be when you preach it.

Be sure also to move your body as you read. A significant amount of oral communication is accomplished by our body language. Start getting your body involved. As you go through your notes, become immersed into the story. Start to feel the emotion that your protagonist felt. Begin to chafe against their conflict. As the process goes on, you will find places in your manuscript that you want to change. It almost feels like your character wants to write his or her own words. As long as the big idea of the story is not being modified, you are OK. Go with the changes. What is happening is not only normal but helpful. Like a tailor custom fitting a suit, you are modifying the details of the story so that they are a perfect fit for your protagonist.

After you have gone through the sermon out loud a couple of times, head back to your office and do a formal rewrite. Remove whatever does not contribute to the tension and highlight your big idea. Enhance what does.

STEP TWELVE | Block your sermon (optional).

If you are new to first-person sermons, skip this step. This is best reserved for more experienced dramatic preachers. If you have preached ten or more first-person sermons, however, you are welcome to give blocking a try. It is an additional step that can increase the effectiveness of all of your sermons.

The technique of blocking comes to us from the stage. Through the centuries, those who practiced the dramatic arts came to realize that different portions of the stage had a different emotional impact on their audience. Nobody really knows why this happens. If you ask an actor for the theory behind blocking, they will probably just shrug and mutter "dramatic convention." We do not know why blocking works, but countless stage performances tell us that it does. We should take the diagram below seriously.[1]

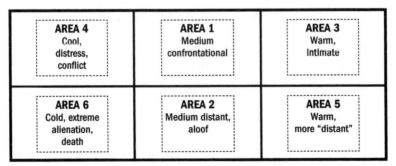

AREA 4 Cool, distress, conflict	AREA 1 Medium confrontational	AREA 3 Warm, Intimate
AREA 6 Cold, extreme alienation, death	AREA 2 Medium distant, aloof	AREA 5 Warm, more "distant"

Whenever you stand on one of the boxes pictured above, you are communicating the mood described within. The boxes are numbered according to the relative strength of the platform. Box 1 is the strongest; box 6 is the weakest.

Most pulpits are placed front and center. This is a confrontational location. If you begin to talk about Christ's love for the church, you may want to move to box 3, the front right of the stage. This area is far more warm and intimate. If you are putting on a passion play, you will want to put the cross in box 6 at the back left. This is where death is felt most keenly. Effective communicators harness the power of the stage by standing in places that complement the particular point that they are making in their sermon. Standing in the right place at the right time automatically makes a sermon more emotionally powerful.

Most preachers do not utilize their platform intentionally. Some stand still and hold onto the pulpit for dear life. Others wander aimlessly. To take your first-person preaching to the next level, I recommend that you take a close look at your final manuscript. As your manuscript changes mood, write the box number of the appropriate place on the stage in the margin. When you rehearse your sermon with manuscript in hand, walk from place to place on the stage. It will not take long for these movements to become second nature. Your movements will become more purposeful as your messages become more powerful.

STEP THIRTEEN | Rehearse your sermon.

When the manuscript editing and blocking is done, get alone and say the sermon aloud with actions. As you become more familiar with your material, put your manuscript aside. Rehearse the revised manuscript two to five times with notes and then two to five times without notes. Work on mastery while standing and moving through the action of the narrative. I do not rehearse Saturday evenings, because if the sermon has the emotion it should, I will deliver it with passion and find it hard to sleep. I want to be well rested on Sunday.

STEP FOURTEEN | Decide about costuming.

Most books on dramatic preaching spend a significant time on costuming. This one won't. You are welcome to dress up. Costuming can enhance the power of your message. If you decide to do so, go professional. Find a place that rents professional period-appropriate, Hollywood-quality costuming. The church is no place for bathrobe drama.

I attended a large church recently where the senior pastor preached a first-person sermon. As he stood to preach, however, it was painfully obvious that someone in the congregation who sewed reasonably well had made his outfit. He was delivering a first-class sermon wearing a third-class outfit. The costume hurt his cause far more than it helped.

The same caution applies to makeup. I have heard and witnessed numerous horror stories of pastors who ventured unsuccessfully into this field. These include fake noses slowly falling off, wigs slipping unnoticed to extraordinarily unnatural angles, and makeup running off in streaks as the lights and heavy costume start the rivers of sweat. At first the listeners are horrified when they notice what is going on. Then the giggles start. It is not long until all of the hard work invested by the preacher is lost. Nobody remembers the big idea of the passage, just the fake nose hanging from the real nose. If you are going to use makeup, get a professional dramatic makeup artist to do it right or do not do it at all.

I have not preached with the assistance of costume or makeup for two reasons. First, once you start preaching with these trappings, you can never go back. Your congregation will expect that you will always use them. You can, of course, always become more elaborate, but if you suddenly decide to take a turn toward simplicity, you will face resistance. It is difficult to stop what you have started. Second, I have never pastored a church that was willing to employ the long-term resources necessary to preach this way. Even if they had been, however, I am not sure that I would have. I am not convinced that it is necessary.

Garrison Keillor is to our generation what Mark Twain was to a previous age: a peerless storyteller. Every week he spins a yarn about the people who inhabit, or have moved away from, Lake Woebegone, Minnesota. He tells these stories with such skill that people are convinced that it actually exists. People drive around St. Paul looking for it. They can't, of course. It doesn't exist. Not physically. But Garrison Keillor does such an outstanding job of painting pictures with words that I can picture that town in my mind's eye. I feel as if I have eaten lunch at the "Chatterbox Cafe," walked past Father Emil's church, "Our Lady of Perpetual Responsibility," and sat next to the Tollerude family in church. His words make the mythical real and the invisible visible. Such is the power of narrative.

First-person sermons have the same potential. We can tap into people's imagination and help them see a distant world with lifelike clarity. If I can stand on a platform in my Sunday suit and have people absolutely convinced that I am Samson, there is no limit to the power of human imagination. I am not sure that a well-told story suffers when I tell it with my own nose.

By all means, use costuming if you have the time, resources, and inclination. Just don't think you must.

STEP FIFTEEN | Deliver your sermon.

Saying the Words

You know your material well enough by now to be able to preach it without notes. So leave your manuscript on your desk. The power of a first-person message lies in the emotional impact and intimacy of one person telling another their testimony. It would seem completely disingenuous for someone to have to refer to notes to describe the most significant event of his or her life. Using notes undercuts the integrity of the message.

When we want to determine if someone is telling the truth, we look him or her in the eyes. We consider a person's eyes to be a window into his or her soul. When we want to know whether our children are lying, we say to them, "Look me in the eye and tell me what happened." Professional interrogators look for unconscious physiological responses, including random eye movement, to determine the truthfulness of a person's statement. If you want your listeners to believe that what your protagonist says is true, look your audience in the eye and talk to them. Are you afraid that you will forget your lines? Don't be. There are two reasons why you can have the confidence to preach this sermon without notes.

First, you should *not* memorize your manuscript. Manuscripting is important because it forces you to think through your message in detail. It makes sure that you have given every portion careful thought and carefully selected the appropriate language. If you try and memorize it, however, you will not only be forced to invest a huge number of hours to get it word perfect (I am not sure I could do it), but you will likely deliver the message in a stilted and unnatural fashion — an unsatisfactory return for the huge amount of work involved! Not the kind of investment I recommend.

Do not memorize your lines. Instead, *internalize your message*! Don't try to get it word perfect. Just speak as the character would. Speak from your heart. You will discover that 80 percent of what you wrote will come back to you word perfect, 10 percent will be better than you wrote, and 10 percent will be worse than you wrote. Don't sweat it. The advantages of improved delivery far outweigh the 10 percent you are obsessing about. You will be most effective when, in the persona of your character, you tell your story in your own words.

The second reason you can preach your first-person sermon without notes is its inherently dramatic structure. I have taught first-person preaching on many occasions and in many locations. Many of these courses lasted only five days. Every single student I have taught has been able to preach a first-person sermon without a note on the fifth day. When I was teaching in the Philippines, I had a Burmese student who had never preached without sitting cross-legged on a mat. On the last day of class, he stood and preached his message like a pro!

Why have all these people been able to remember their sermons? Because if you do the work that I have been outlining, the narrative structure is almost impossible to forget. Preaching a narrative is as easy as riding a toboggan. You sit at the top of the mono-mythic cycle of your sermon structure as if it were a snow-covered hill. And with a little nudge in your introduction to get moving, you simply let narrative gravity pull you toward the bottom of the cycle. The dynamic tension of a good story will pull you all the way down. If your story is coherent and has tension (and you have done the hard exegetical work that I have outlined), your story is almost impossible to forget.

If you happen to get stuck, don't panic. You get moving again the same way you would in a toboggan. Walk back up the hill a bit and take another run at it. Just back up your story to where you remember it clearly and start heading down toward the climax of your story again! You will break through the memory block like a toboggan through a snow drift!

Take the plunge. Speak the message of your protagonist the way that your protagonist would. Look the audience in the eyes and speak truth from the heart. Let the vocal and physical response come from within and be appropriate for the character you are presenting. Do not be afraid of pauses. Most beginners talk too fast. Where possible, videotape your sermon and watch it a few weeks later to see how you did.

Becoming the Person

Far more important than what you are wearing when you preach is whether or not you genuinely "get into" your character when you preach the sermon. Preaching a first-person sermon is not the same as preaching "three points and a poem." In a first-person sermon, you do not stand outside of your message and reflect abstractly about the ramifications of the big idea of your passage. Instead, you climb out of your life into the life of your protagonist. You personally embody the big idea of the text. What happens to your character literally happens to you.

Work hard at becoming your character. For this message, you must emotionally become one with the character you created. When their child dies, you are bereaved. When they are betrayed, you are personally devastated. When you first stride out onto the platform as Samson, you are as arrogant as the day is long. By the end of the sermon, however, you are a broken shadow of your former self, gripped by remorse for having traded away a lifetime of ministry effectiveness for a moment of sin. When you look at your listeners with eyes genuinely moist with remorse and say "Don't make the mistake that I made. Nobody sins and gets away with it. Not me. Not you."

To preach this way, you must leave your pride at home. You cannot preserve your dignity and preach an effective first-person expository sermon. I have never preached a first-person sermon without experiencing a measure of embarrassment. What is a respected professor and pastor doing acting like this? It hardly seems dignified. I have to battle with my pride every time I preach a first-person message.

Why do I do it? Because I know that in these messages people clearly hear the Word of God. My goal in life is to change people's lives with the Word of God and to help others do the same. I am willing to do anything short of sin to clearly communicate God's Word. It is this perspective that allows me to genuinely connect with my protagonist and communicate his message with genuine abandon. You will never preach first-person sermons well unless your supreme desire is to communicate the big idea of the text.

NOTES FOR CHAPTER SIX

1. Reg Grant and John Reed, *Telling Stories to Touch the Heart* (Wheaton: Victor, 1990), 68.

PART THREE

QUESTIONS AND ALTERNATIVES

Chapter Seven

PRACTICAL QUESTIONS ABOUT FIRST-PERSON PREACHING

After a recent weekend speaking engagement in Detroit, I entered into a lively early morning conversation with the Avis shuttle bus driver taking me to the terminal. During the six-minute bus ride, this driver displayed an impressive knowledge of the airport and those who used it. He not only knew what airlines flew out of what terminals, but how many people flew to what destinations. He also knew how and why the passenger numbers varied during the year. I was impressed. He really seemed to have a handle on flying out of Detroit. You can imagine my surprise, therefore, when the shuttle bus driver told me that in the seventeen years he had driven the route, he had never flown or even walked inside of one of the terminals. "No not once," he said. "All I ever do is drive to the curb."

I want you to get beyond the curb, to take your preaching further. I want you to see the look of wonderment in people's eyes as they experience the old, old stories for the very first time. I want you to see them shout with excitement as David slays Goliath and to hear them weep as Barabbas witnesses Jesus dying in his place. I want you to experience the thrill of preaching effective expository first-person sermons.

Why are we tempted to stay on the bus? To preach from the curb? Sometimes it's because we have never seen one. The reason this book includes a CD-ROM is to allow you to experience a first-person sermon firsthand. It is also why appendix 1 includes three sample sermons. Take the time to look at how some preachers have tried to do what you have been reading about. Note their differences. Although each sermon faithfully communicates the Scriptures, each is as unique as the personalities of the people who preached them. Learn from these preachers, but don't merely parrot them. The sermons that communicate authorial intent most effectively will reflect your personality. Be who you are while saying what God said.

Other times we stay on the bus because we have some genuine questions we need to have answered. So let me provide some answers to frequently asked questions.

QUESTION ONE | Does it take longer to prepare a first-person sermon?

Yes and no. The exegetical work required for a first-person sermon is the same as for a "regular" sermon. Regardless of the sermon style you select, you must understand your passage. How long it takes to identify the big idea of the passage is dependent on your level of exegetical skill and the difficulty of the passage you have selected.

I have found that narrative passages resemble the nuts that my wife always puts out during the Christmas season. Some of those nuts, like some passages, have soft shells that are quickly opened and easily yield their flesh. Other nuts are small and tough. They resist my futile efforts, escape from my nutcracker, fall on the floor, and try to hide under the sofa. I retrieve the wayward nut, take it to my workroom, and after having secured it in my oversized vice, begin to pound it with a framing hammer. These tough nuts do give up their flesh, but not without a lot of effort. Some biblical passages put up a similar fight, but not all.

Does the homiletical task take longer with a first-person sermon? It will at the beginning. The first few times you preach a first-person message you should allow some extra hours. As with any skill, there is a learning curve to writing first-person sermons. You can flatten this curve by studying the examples provided for you in appendix 1 and listening to my sample sermon, but the first half-dozen sermons will take more time to write. Eventually, however, you will find that first-person messages take only slightly longer to prepare than a "typical" message.

QUESTION TWO | How should I introduce first-person preaching to my church?

Some preachers pray primarily for strength. Not me. I have learned that successful ministry requires far more than muscle. Samson proved that. Samson had more energy at his disposal than the rest of us combined. What he lacked was the wisdom to use it well. We have to work smart, not just hard. This includes knowing how to best introduce first-person sermons into your ministry context. Usually congregations accept this type of preaching instantly and over-whelmingly, though not always.

A few years ago, as a visiting preacher, I preached a first-person to a conservative New England church. The reaction of the congregation was almost 99 percent positive. But it was not 100 percent. A few people objected, and did so strongly. Two of the most outspoken men protested that a dramatic presentation of an Old Testament character was "inappropriate" and "disrespectful." The very next day they proceeded to act out the life of Christ with hand puppets in a vacation Bible school program! Go figure.

On another occasion, in a church where I was the senior pastor, an elderly gentleman came to my office and, after a very pleasant conversation, accused me of using "Jim Jones" manipulation techniques by preaching first-person sermons. He was mystified by my narrative approach because "you can preach regular sermons real good."

Not everyone will think you are a genius. Even the finest leaders in Scripture faced "friendly fire," but they didn't go looking for it either. Here is a strategy to consider if you suspect that you may face resistance. As you do, pray for wisdom.

Calvin and Hobbes ©1993 Watterson. Reprinted with permission of Universal Press Syndicate. All rights reserved.

Begin by preaching a first-person sermon to your church's youth group at an event held away from the main church campus. If you hear positive feedback from your first foray into the dramatic, try a second time to the youth. This time, however, deliver your dramatic sermon at a non-Sunday event held on the main church campus. By this time, if you have worked hard on these first two messages, a positive buzz will probably be spreading throughout the church. If it is, feel free to preach a first-person sermon to the adults at a nonworship service event such as a Christmas or Valentine's Day banquet. If things go well, you should have the freedom to preach a first-person sermon on a Sunday morning service in the sanctuary.

You may also want to consider some of the alternate narrative homiletical options outlined in chapter 8. First-person sermons are an effective and winsome way to communicate the narratives of Scripture, but they are not the only way. While you don't want to run away from every possible criticism, no sermon form is worth your ministry. You will not be able to influence a church that fires you.

QUESTION THREE | How should I begin a first-person sermon?

I have had the privilege of planting a church and serving as its senior pastor for almost a decade. As I preached first-person sermons through those years, I discovered that it is prudent to orient people to this unique sermon form, even when the congregation is familiar with them. Here is a typical preface that I may give before delivering a first-person sermon.

> One of my passions in life is the study of preaching. I want to learn how to clearly, faithfully, and relevantly preach the Word of God. In my office, I have shelves of books on preaching. While each of those books has contributed in some way to my understanding of the subject, there is one book that has shaped my understanding of preaching far more than any other. This book. The Bible. And of all the preachers recorded on its pages, the one who stands above all others is the person of Jesus Christ. He is the peerless preacher.
>
> When you examine the sermons of Christ recorded in Scripture, however, it is interesting to note how often Jesus chose to preach in story form. He knew that stories have a wonderful way of capturing our attention and sneaking past our defenses as they communicate the words of God. This morning, with your permission, I would like to take a page out of Jesus' homiletical textbook. I would like to preach the kind of sermon that Jesus might preach if he were here this morning. I would like to preach a "first-person" sermon—a message in which I become a character who participated in a biblical story and tell you that person's story in his own words.
>
> While not every detail I present comes directly from the pages of Scripture, every detail has been thoroughly researched and is historically, culturally, and socially consistent with that day and the intent of the passage.
>
> You are welcome to turn in your Bible to 1 Samuel 16–17 and follow along with me in the text, or you can just sit back, listen, and relive the events of Scripture through the eyes of someone who was there.

At this point, I back up two or three feet and slowly turn around (360 degrees). When I am facing the audience once again, I am in character. I have transitioned into the protagonist of my sermon. The sermon has begun.

While rotating may seem an unusual transitioning tool, it is very helpful. When you turn 360 degrees, you are communicating to your congregation in a visual, dramatic way that everything has changed — and something entirely new is about to begin.

QUESTION FOUR | Should I read the biblical text before the sermon?

Paul urges us in 1 Timothy 4:13 to "devote yourself to the public reading of Scripture, to preaching and to teaching." We cannot give up the public reading of the Word of God. At the same time, however, you will want to think through the way in which you will read Scripture those weeks that you preach a first-person sermon. This is an issue for two reasons.

First, most first-person messages are based on long passages of Scripture. Many of the biblical narratives you will be preaching exceed two chapters. Some go on for many more. Time limitations of the typical worship service often make it impossible to both read and preach a complete biblical narrative.

A second reason for carefully considering how you will read Scripture is the element of tension. Tension, as we have already seen, is one of the most important components of a first-person sermon. Without tension, you have no story, sermon, or interest. To give away the ending of your story through the reading of the biblical text immediately before you preach your sermon is counterproductive. You hurt your own cause. Your ambition is to withhold the surprising twist and maintain tension as long as possible, not give it away in advance. There are at least two ways that you can read Scripture in the context of first-person preaching.

First, you could choose not to read the narrative you are preaching. Instead, you could perhaps read an alternative portion of Scripture that deals with the subject addressed in your passage. This can be effective if the passage you select asks questions or otherwise raises needs without positing a solution.

Alternatively, you could read selected portions of your narrative text — only those portions that set up the story and begin to build the tension. Under no circumstances, however, should you read the "best part" of the story. Do not reveal the complement of your narrative by reading the "twist in the plot." This relieves the tension of your sermon as effectively as a pin relieves the pressure of a blown-up balloon.

QUESTION FIVE | How much extrabiblical material should be added to a sermon?

This is a good question. A bad question is, "*Should* I add extrabiblical material to a sermon." Of course you should add extrabiblical material. All sermon forms contain extrabiblical material. Even the preachers recorded in Scripture added to the biblical text. A sermon, by definition, must go beyond the mere recitation or regurgitation of biblical texts. They must extrapolate and expound on the Scriptures.

It is entirely legitimate to include extrabiblical material to any sermon form *as long as this material gives the listener a clearer understanding of the authorial intent* of the passage. It is, of course, appropriate for you to add relevant historical and cultural material. You must tell your listeners explicitly what the original audience would have known implicitly.

In addition, however, it is also appropriate to tease legitimate psychological and physical implications out of the text. You must get beyond viewing the Bible in an exclusively objective, sterile, scientific sense. The pages of Scripture are populated by people who felt the same emotions of life that we do.

In Luke 9:28–36, for example, we read that Peter, James, and John witnessed the transfiguration of Jesus. As Christ was praying, the "appearance of his face changed, and his clothes became as bright as a flash of lightning. Two men, Moses and Elijah, appeared in glorious splendor, talking with Jesus." A few minutes later, a voice said, "This is my Son, whom I have chosen; listen to him."

What emotions were the three disciples experiencing through this episode? The text does not explicitly tell us. You need to use the available evidence and extrapolate. If you were one of the three disciples, how would you have responded? Bored or blasé? I doubt it. I think that we (and they) would have been experiencing a crash course in what it really means to fear God! I am sure they were both terrified and awestruck by what they had experienced. It is legitimate to draw out the natural psychological inferences of a biblical text. As you do, you help your audience enter into a fuller, more intimate understanding of this passage.

The touchstone for the biblical preacher is authorial intent. Ask yourself: "Does this information give my congregation a deeper understanding and appreciation of the original writer's purpose for this passage?" If it does, include it. If it doesn't, lay the information aside. Authorial intent is what holds you to orthodoxy. If you are not anchored to the authorial intent of a passage, you are theologically adrift. This commitment to say only and all that God said in a passage of Scripture is what distinguishes a biblical preacher from a false prophet. Commit yourself to say what God said — no more, no less.

QUESTION SIX | Do I need background training in drama?

Since first-person sermons are inherently dramatic, an understanding of the dramatic arts can be helpful. At the same time, however, you are not excluded from first-person preaching if you have never been bathed in footlights. This homiletical form is not restricted to the few thespians among us. I was not involved in drama in high school or college. You can do it! Don't let your lack of stage experience intimidate you. Here is what you need to step off the curb and try this homiletical form.

Begin by visualizing the biblical story. Your exegetical goal is to "see" the story you are preaching — to lift the narrative off the paper and create an accurate mental motion picture out of the biblical material. You need to "watch" Ruth gleaning in the fields of Boaz.

- What kind of clothes is she wearing?
- How is she likely wearing her hair?
- What tools is she using?
- How many harvesters does Boaz have?
- What time of the year is it?
- What temperature is it likely to be?
- What is the topography of the area?
- How unusual is it for Boaz to tell his men to deliberately leave grain in the field for her to pick up?

Good research is critical in the creation of good drama. Do you think that John Grisham studied the judicial system before writing *Runaway Jury*? Did Sebastian Junger have to learn a thing or two about commercial fishing before writing *The Perfect Storm*? Of course. The details that these authors discovered during their study make their stories interesting and believable. If you want the results, you have to do the work. The rule of thumb with first-person sermons is: "If you can see the story, your audience will see it. If it is real to you, it will be real to them."

Second, you need to "feel" the biblical story. Use your sanctified imagination to climb into the world and life of the biblical characters. Feel what they felt. Imagine how they would have responded in various situations. Make sure you understand their motivation — why they did what they did. What was their goal? What personal need would they be satisfying by reaching this objective? You cannot portray a person you do not understand.

Third, you need to be willing to embody your protagonist as you deliver your sermon. To achieve first-person authenticity in the pulpit, you must exchange your persona for your characters. You become that person. This is impossible to achieve unless you are willing to set your pride aside. If polishing a professional pastoral image is most important to you, do not even try to preach first-person sermons. Prideful delivery will make you look like a badly handled string puppet, not a person significantly used by the living God.

These steps will help you deliver powerful first-person sermons regardless of your dramatic background. Use them to preach some of the most influential sermons of your ministry.

QUESTION SEVEN | What if I am not very creative?

Who is? The most creative people I know were not born that way. What creative people do have in common, however, is a commitment to do the hard work necessary to be creative. Anyone who understands and applies the principles of creativity can achieve extraordinary results. You can be far more creative. Here's how.

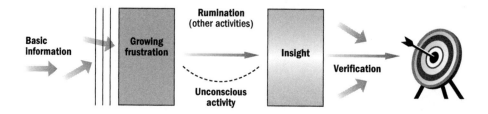

Creativity begins with basic information. In sermon preparation, the basic information you need is the big idea. You must start with the hard exegetical work of stage 1. After you have written out your exegetical, homiletical, and preaching ideas, you can begin the daunting task of determining the best way to communicate the idea and then creating it. Here is where preachers often run into problems. They are not sure what to do or how to do it best. Many of their early ideas seem fraught with problems or rehashed clichés. There is growing frustration.

At this point students typically ask if they can select another passage to exegete. "Surely," they think, "all of these difficulties will be resolved if I have another — easier — passage to work with." *Very rarely is this true*. Only a beginning narrative preacher who has selected a passage far beyond his or her abilities should start again with a new passage. In every other situation, the best approach is simply to shoulder on. The frustration you feel is not a signal to give up on your passage. Frustration is a signal that you have moved on to the next stage of the creative process. It is an integral part of the creative process. You need to develop a love-hate relationship with it.

After working on the homiletical problem for a significant number of hours, the best thing to do is to take a break. Do something entirely different. Go for a jog, cut the grass, build some bookshelves, vacuum the house, wash the car, anything. Just leave your books and do something completely dissimilar. The third stage of the creative process is largely unconscious. It arises from the rumination that occurs in the background when your mind is occupied with a different, less intellectually rigorous task. It is amazing how often the best, most creative insights come "out of the blue" while you are thinking about other things, or how frequently people wake up in the night with a wonderful solution that had plagued them while awake.

Next, verify the integrity of this newfound insight. Make sure that your solution actually solves your problem. If it does, you know that you have discovered the solution you have been looking for. The creativity you wanted has arrived.

Everyone can be creative — even you! All it takes is the self-discipline to begin the process early enough to allow for rumination. If you give yourself the luxury of time, you will find yourself becoming much more creative. Start your preparation early. "Saturday Night Specials" result in desperate preaching, not creative exposition. Give yourself a break. Give yourself the time you need.

Calvin and Hobbes ©1993 Watterson. Reprinted with permission of Universal Press Syndicate. All rights reserved.

QUESTION EIGHT | What are the hardest passages to preach?

The ones that you know the best. If you grew up in the church, you have heard some Bible stories countless times — in Sunday school, youth group, Awana, and summer camp and from the pulpit. Every time you heard those stories, an idea was communicated. Implicitly or explicitly, the storyteller told you what it meant. What they said may have correctly represented the authorial intent of the original writer, or they may not have. But when we hear the same stories associated with the same ideas hundreds of times, the association between the story and its interpretation becomes strong. We don't have to think about what a story means. Right or wrong, we have memorized it.

The temptation we face in stage 1 of our sermon preparation is passing on old teaching without reevaluating the biblical text for ourselves. When we do minimal exegesis on familiar passages, we can end up preaching clichés — regurgitating the familiar lines of yesteryear — without giving them the original thought they deserve.

Preconceived opinions encrusted with tradition are difficult to overcome. To preach a fresh word to a new generation, however, we must be willing to question and reexamine even the most familiar exegetical terrain.

QUESTION NINE | How important is humor?

Humor is frequently underestimated as a communication tool. On the surface, it appears light, frothy, irrelevant, and perhaps irreverent. Like an iceberg, however, its most influential feature rests beneath the surface. Humor's power lies in its ability to create a sense of identification. Whenever you laugh at a joke, you are, on some level, identifying with its message. A measure of agreement hides within the folds of our giggles. That explains why we belly laugh when Bill Cosby talks about his misadventures at the dentist's office — we know how hard it is to spit with half our mouth frozen with Novocain. It also explains why we cannot laugh at a dirty joke — we cannot endorse the value system that lies beneath the humor.

When your listeners laugh with and at your character, they are identifying with your character. The greater the identification, the greater the impact that the big idea (which the character embodies) will have on the lives of the listeners. Humor is not the only way that your audience can bond with the audience, but it can be a very effective way.

Calvin and Hobbes ©1986 Watterson.
Reprinted with permission of Universal Press Syndicate. All rights reserved.

QUESTION TEN | How often should I preach a first-person sermon?

On average, I preach four to six first-person sermons a year. My goal is to use this homiletical option only when it is the best way to communicate a specific passage to a specific audience. The rest of the time, I use one of the narrative homiletical alternatives outlined in chapter 8.

Why do I select a first-person sermon some weeks and not others? Sometimes I select a first-person sermon because of the emotion of my text. First-person sermons are your best homiletical option to express raw emotion. When you want to preach a narrative that is overflowing with emotion, you cannot make a better choice.

Other times I choose to preach in the first person because of the familiarity of the text. First-person sermons are a great way to help your congregation catch a renewed glimpse of a familiar narrative. This is why I always preach first-person messages at Christmas and Easter. The accounts of Jesus' birth and death are wonderful, emotionally rich stories, but their familiarity can make our sermons sound as stale and unappealing as last year's fruitcake. If you have pastored in the same church for a few years, you know how hard it is to come up with fresh Christmas and Easter sermons. With first-person sermons, however, you have far more options. There are as many possibilities as there are characters around the cross and the manger.

QUESTION ELEVEN | What about application?

If emotion is the strength of this homiletical form, application is its weakness — a weakness formed by the limited cultural awareness of the character telling the story. When an ancient character tells us their story, we are immediately caught up in their world. We learn where the biblical characters lived, worshiped, worked, and fought. The biblical characters, however, do not learn the same level of detail about our lives. They are strangers to our age.

If you were developing a first-person sermon featuring Jacob's son Joseph, it would be appropriate for your Joseph to display an in-depth understanding of the Egyptian prison system. This would be entirely consistent with our understanding of the character and the rules of this homiletical genre established in your introduction. It would not, however, be appropriate for your Joseph character to refer to the baseball rivalry that exists between the Boston Red Sox and the New York Yankees, even if it generates some laughs. If you give your character an unrealistic awareness of the contemporary world, you will compromise the integrity of this homiletical genre and reduce its ability to influence your listeners. When your character acts and speaks in ways inconsistent with reality, you make a mockery of yourself and your pulpit.

How much contemporary awareness can you give your character? Here is my rule of thumb. Do you remember the original *Star Trek* TV series? You can only give your first-person characters the same level of cultural awareness that a member of an "away team" would have when they "beamed down to an unknown planet." Or, to change the metaphor, they can be as culturally aware as you would be if you just stepped off a single engine plane this afternoon in Mount Hagen, Papua New Guinea. Not much.

This limited contemporary awareness has obvious implications on how the character can apply the biblical text to the lives of the listeners. On the positive side, this character can speak the main idea of their experience directly to the listeners. They can look the listeners in the eye and state the homiletical and preaching ideas with a blunt intensity reserved for those who have learned a lesson the hard way. Don't underrate the impact this can make. It is potent communication, but it is not specific.

The weakness of the first-person sermon form is its inability to apply the homiletical and preaching ideas of the sermon to the details of the lives of the listeners. Samson can say, "Don't sin!" but he cannot say, "Don't sin by surfing to pornographic websites on the internet," or "Don't sin by using ecstasy at a rave." Samson simply cannot have access to this information.

One of the ways that you can compensate for this is to have someone come after you have finished saying "Don't sin!" and do the application for you. If you decide to do this:

- Realize that the secondary application will have much less emotional power than the first-person sermon itself.
- Remember to keep this very short. The story is over. The tension is gone. Interest has almost totally dissipated.
- Write it out. Don't trust specific application to spur of the moment inspiration. Write down what you want this other person to say. Include them in your final preparation.

It is rare, however, that I have had others apply my message. I find that when you make your homiletical and preaching ideas with dramatic intensity and clarity, it is relatively easy for listeners to make the specific concrete applications called for in the text.

Twenty years ago I was a new, very green pastor in my first full-time church: a small, conservative, rural congregation. As I left the house to go jogging one morning, I popped a *Preaching Today* cassette into my Walkman. What followed changed my preaching. As I ran through the barren countryside, I was captivated by what I was hearing. My first first-person sermon. I had never heard anything like this. The concept both fascinated and terrified me. But I could not let it alone, so much so that I decided to try and preach one the following week. To be honest, I really didn't know what I was doing. I certainly didn't have the benefit of the chapters you have just read! I fully realized the risk I was taking about half an hour before the worship service began. It was then that I began to panic.

"What am I doing?" I asked myself. "What kind of crazy risk am I taking? I have never seen anyone do anything like this! How will the congregation respond? Will they run me out of town? Is my young career about to end?" I was so afraid that I began shaking like a leaf. At that moment, if I could have, I would have gone back to my office, dusted off an old sermon, and preached it. But I was just starting out in ministry. I had no sermons in my barrel. I was stuck!

It was lack of alternatives rather than courage that propelled me to the pulpit that morning. I must have been as white as a sheet when I took on the character of Aquila from Acts 18 and began to talk about how wonderful it was to share in the ministry of the apostle Paul with my wife, Priscilla.

I am sure that I did many things wrong that morning. I know that it was not a perfect sermon. But what surprised me the most was the response of the people. They loved it! The response was overwhelming. When I resigned from the church some years later, this was one of the sermons that people singled out to thank me for! I would never have enriched their lives and expanded my homiletical horizons if I had not taken the risk that morning.

Get off the bus! Preach a first-person sermon!

Chapter Eight

NARRATIVE ALTERNATIVES TO FIRST-PERSON PREACHING

My Utmost for His Highest — the title of Oswald Chambers' classic book has always inspired me. It expresses what I want to do with my life. Like you, I want to honor God by doing my best — even in the pulpit. But how?

A common complaint I hear from students entering their Doctor of Ministry studies is: "I am bored by my own preaching." This complaint is made all the more astonishing because it comes from men and women who have labored in the church for a decade or more and who are deeply in love with God and his Word. These servants of God work with diligence every week in an attempt to be faithful to the Scriptures and relevant to their audience. They don't want to be boring — but they are. Their congregations say so.

Why? How can such exciting stories end up on Sunday mornings as bland as a beige wall? One reason that preachers preach boring messages is repetition.

What is your favorite meal? Pizza? Kimchi? Sushi? No matter how much you enjoy a particular food, you wouldn't want to eat it at every meal. One of the surest ways to reduce your affinity for a particular food is to eat it too often. Repetition can transform outstanding into less than ordinary. This mistake can be made in the pulpit as well as the kitchen.

Many well-meaning preachers use the same preaching method that they learned in seminary over and over again — week after week, decade after decade. At least in general terms they know what they are going to say at 11:35 a.m. on any given Sunday morning until retirement. They are as formulaic as a rhythm machine, and just about as inspiring. But they don't venture into the unorthodox for fear of saying something wrong. I admire their desire for theological orthodoxy but grow frustrated with their lack of originality. It is time to try a new recipe, to serve up the Word of God in ways that are appetizing as well as nourishing.

I heard of a young man who took his father's new car to an old gravel pit to see what the car could do without being bothered by anyone — without permission. He was having great fun until he lost control on a high speed turn, flipped the car, and pinned himself behind the wheel. But this was not the worst of it. It seems that when the car turned over, his father's favorite music cassette, which had been sitting in the player, got sucked into the stereo system and began playing, endlessly. The young man could not turn it off and it took most of a day for the car to be noticed and the rescue team to pry him out.

I never heard how the father punished his disobedient son. Maybe he didn't. Being forced to listen to "old man's" music over and over again could be considered cruel and unusual punishment. Those who listen to our sermons may agree. It is time for us to expand our repertoire. Learn a new tune or two.

Repetition, however, is not the only cause of boring sermons. Boring sermons also occur when preachers do not match the homiletical form of their message to the literary form of the passage being preached. As I noted in chapter 1, God communicated his Word by equally inspiring the very words and genres that he knew were appropriate for his purposes. The idea of a biblical text is communicated through inspired words arranged in an inspired literary form. This combination of inspired words and genres is adequate to communicate God's ideas — and must be respected by the contemporary preacher.

The literary format used to transmit the message is an integral part of the message itself. Expository preachers must allow both the words and the genre of a biblical text to influence their messages. If the homiletical form that a preacher utilizes in Sunday's sermon is significantly different from the literary form that God originally used in the Bible, then the sermon will not accurately communicate the biblical text, no matter how long the preacher has labored in the study. A homiletical form that is not genre appropriate will distort the meaning of the text and strip it of its inherent literary power.

The Bible we carry to the pulpit is a portable library. It features wonderfully diverse literature, which should be preached just as diversely. There is no one "proper" form that a sermon should take. Our homiletical forms can be as creative as God himself is. Since our goal is to faithfully retransmit previously inspired literature, the form of the inspired literature needs to govern the creativity of our preaching. God communicated each of his ideas with the most appropriate literary form. We need to follow his example. Epistles should be preached with homiletical forms that reflect the unique elements of that genre. So should the narratives. Extending the literary form of a biblical text into the form of your sermon will allow you to communicate his word more accurately.

But this is not all. When you match the form of your sermon to the form of your passage, you capture its rhetorical power. Just as a hydroelectric dam harnesses the power of a river, so genre-appropriate sermon forms harness the literary power of the original passage. Your sermon is more likely to have the same impact on your listeners that the original text had on its listeners if you use the form it used.

When we preach one of the great stories of Scripture as abstract points, we suck the dramatic life out of them. We kill the story by conducting a homiletical autopsy — cutting it up and exposing its various parts one at a time to our congregation. As we do this, our listeners slide into terminal boredom. It is a sin to bore people with the Word of God. If you want to have the same impact on your listeners as the original author had on the original audience, then echo the form of the original text in your sermon form.

Narrative Appropriate Characteristics

Narrative texts are preached most accurately and powerfully when they are preached narratively. How do we do this?

No definitive list of "proper" narrative homiletical forms has been approved by an international symposium of homileticians. You are welcome to creatively construct your own narrative forms. I suggest, however, that all narrative homiletic forms share the following four characteristics.

- *Tension.* Narratives are arranged inductively around a single idea. The level of tension experienced by the audience escalates as the intensity of the conflict experienced by the protagonist in the story increases until either the story ends tragically or, because of a surprising twist in the plot, has a happy conclusion. Narrative sermons will also be arranged inductively and move inexorably, as the conflict increases, toward a single idea. They can have either a tragic or comedic resolution.
- *Concretism.* In biblical narratives, abstract ideas are always presented and discussed in physical, tangible, "real-life" form. Paul discusses the doctrine of justification by faith in his letter to the Romans. Abraham demonstrates the doctrine of justification by faith in the narrative of Genesis. Narrative sermons demonstrate rather than discuss a truth.
- *Emotion.* The stories of Scripture touched the hearts as well as the minds of the people who heard them. Narrative sermons make their point emotionally. Listeners "feel" that they understand the idea of the sermon.
- *Literary artistry.* Biblical narratives are not rough-hewn yarns. They were written with inspired skill and excellence, the archetype of

human literature. Narrative sermons reflect the same level of excellence. They are not an optional shortcut during a particularly busy week of ministry.

Any sermon form that includes tension, concretism, emotion, and literary artistry is appropriate to use with narrative literature. Such a message will effectively retransmit the authorial intent of narrative literature to your congregation and protect you from the sin of the homiletical humdrum.

Effective preachers want to approach a narrative text with a number of homiletical options. During stage 1 of their sermon preparation, they go through their exegetical work without consideration of the homiletical challenges that lie ahead. After using the big idea of the text as a key to pass into stage 2, the homiletical phase, however, effective preachers demand the widest possible range of homiletical options. They want to have a quiver full of alternatives from which to select the one that will best communicate a particular text to a particular audience on a particular occasion.

No homiletical form is perfect. All sermonic forms have inherent advantages and disadvantages. Wise preachers will, therefore, collect and develop the widest array of homiletical forms possible. Like a good mechanic, good preachers want the most extensive tool selection possible. This helps them do the best work possible.

Alternatives to First-Person Sermons

In addition to first-person sermons, what follows in this chapter is a description of some narrative genre-appropriate homiletical alternatives.

Homiletical Plot

Eugene Lowry's[1] unique sermon outline was revolutionary when introduced back in 1980, and it can still be used with effect today. This homiletical outline is not traditional. It is neither linear or syllogistic. Its design does, however, allow you to emphasize the tension and resolution of a biblical narrative.

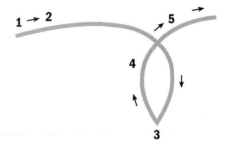

In Lowry's sermon outline, point 1 is *the upsetting of the equilibrium* or status quo. Point 2 is given to an *examination of the discrepancy* between the ideal past and the less-than-ideal present. It is not until point 3 that *the clue to resolution* (the complement of the big idea of the text) is finally disclosed. Briefly, at the conclusion of the message, Lowry encourages preachers in point 4 to help their audiences to *experience the difference* that the gospel makes in the listener's situation. The sermon ends in point 5 with the audience *anticipating the consequences* that this new information will make in the future. (Or, as Lowry's students shorthanded this outline: 1–Oops; 2–Ugh; 3–Aha; 4–Whee; 5–Yeah.)

As you think through "the loop," you may notice that what Lowry proposed is not very different from the mono-mythic cycle we have discussed at length elsewhere. The inciting event disturbs perfection — *oops!* The majority of the sermon descends emotionally downward as it examines the growing tension or discrepancy between how things are and what they once were — *ugh!* The visual twist in the plot occurs when the clue to resolution, or big idea, of the text is revealed — *aha!* From this point onward, the mood is moving upward toward an emotionally satisfying or comedic ending.

The most significant and lasting contribution of Lowry's loop is his insight into why and how to get from the dead of the mono-mythic's winter back to summer. To do this, he recommends you take time to revel in the wonder of the good news of the big idea of the text — *whee!* Then think ahead. How will the truth of this text change the trajectory of your life? What long-term difference will it make? — *yeah!* Lowry's loop remains a viable option for those preachers who want to match the genre of a narrative text with an appropriate sermon form.

Life Shaping

A second alternative to first-person preaching is what I have called "Life Shaping." Every preacher knows that people love to listen to sermons on the people of Scripture. Life Shaping gives you a narrative genre-sensitive approach to biographical preaching. It is an alternative to the "history review and lessons learned" approach so frequently employed.

The premise is quite simple. After helping your congregation understand *why* the heroes of Scripture made the decisions they did and *what* the consequences were, it will encourage them to *choose* whether to follow or avoid their example. This is accomplished by intertwining the lives of your listeners with the lives of the characters of Scripture. It harnesses the narrative power of Scripture, as the diagram below suggests, by utilizing the Bible's mono-mythic cycle. As your congregation revisits the six phases of a biblical character's life, they are encouraged to avoid the bad decisions and emulate the positive choices. It helps people reshape their lives by helping them make better decisions. Let me explain in detail using Daniel 1 as an illustration of how this could be done.

1. Personal identification with biblical character.

Your sermon begins in the "summer" of the narrative. Your goal in this portion of the sermon is to help your audience identify with the biblical character. Build bridges between the biblical character and your audience. You want your audience to discover the ways in which their lives are linked to the lives of the biblical character. It may be helpful to ask yourself:

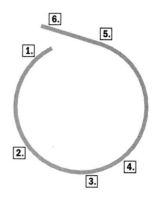

- Who is this person?
- Where does he or she live?
- What is his or her background, education level, profession, and social standing?
- In what ways is this biblical character like my audience?

2. Cultivate the awareness that characters in stories (biblical and contemporary) can and must make choices.

As you relate the "fall" difficulties being faced by the biblical character, show the parallel pressures in the life of your congregation. Biblical characters were real people. You want your congregation to "feel" the same tension and pressure that the biblical hero felt leading up to her or his decision. Harness this pressure to help your audience recognize that we cannot avoid making choices. The following questions will help clarify your thoughts.

- Is the biblical character a victim or a victimizer? Of whom or of what?
- Does the character display a sense of powerlessness?
- Have you (or someone you know) ever felt the same way?

> Daniel does not try to create a conflict with his superiors. He simply desires to live a life in obedience to his God. Yet, he is directed by his superiors to act in a way that would violate the clear commands of his God. Should Daniel keep peace and eat the food set before him, or should he jeopardize his life and career by standing firm on ancient laws made in a faraway land?
>
> What options does Daniel have? Do you ever face situations similar to Daniel's? Are you tempted to go with the culture and compromise on clear but costly portions of God's Word? What options do you think you have in those situations?
>
> In Daniel 1, the hero is a person like us. Daniel is living (whether he wants to or not) in an overwhelmingly secular environment that is hostile to his faith. Have you ever felt like a helpless pawn in a God-hating work environment?

3. Help your congregation to understand *what* the biblical character decided and *why* he or she made these choices.

At this point, you are in the winter of the biblical story. Things have become unbearable and the character has chosen to act. You are at the bottom of the mono-mythic circle, the climax of the emotion. Here you are looking for the biblical character's psychological motivation.

- What would have made this decision difficult?
- When did the character finally choose to act?
- Why not earlier or later?
- What decision did this person make?
- Why did he or she finally choose to act?
- What factors motivated this individual to act the way he or she did (e.g., social, physical, spiritual, etc.)?

> Daniel must choose whether to obey the king of Babylon or the King of kings. Daniel chooses to obey God over human authority, and to do so in the least offensive way possible. He sets up an experiment to show that God's laws are good laws. He demonstrates that being obedient to God is both a smart decision and a sanctified decision. What is Daniel's motivation? It is to honor God without needlessly antagonizing his ungodly superiors.

Note that for this sermon to be biblical, your understanding of the biblical character's choice *must* come from the text itself. Your responsibility as a preacher is to help your congregation understand the message that the original author intended his audience to learn. Preaching the right sermon form enables you to unleash the literary dynamic of God's Word. Preaching the right big idea enables you to unleash the purpose of God into the lives of your congregation.

4. Help your congregation emotionally identify with the consequences that biblical characters faced as a result of their choices.

At phase 4, the diagram above curves upward. It assumes that you are preaching a biblical story that has a happy ending. These "comedic" stories are best used to show audiences how godly decisions result in restored lives.

Not all stories end as positively as the story in Daniel 1. Characters such as Samson, Saul, and Absalom did not make God-honoring decisions. The lesson of their lives is helpful but negative. We must therefore show our listeners the benefit of *not* imitating their decisions.

Regardless of whether the biblical narrative you are preaching ends up or down, you need to help your congregation slip into the sandals of the biblical character that just made the decision. God-honoring decisions have a real and often immediate impact on the life story of the decision maker. Allow your congregation to see this.

- What happened to the character when the choice was made?
- What happened to those around the character (i.e., friends, family, members of the community)?

- If the character could have gone back in time and rewritten the story, do you think that he or she would have made a different decision?
- Have you ever faced/made a similar decision to the biblical character? Did you face similar consequences? Why?
- Would the consequences experienced by the biblical character likely follow a similar decision today? Why?

> Look at what happened to Daniel. He passed the test! There was good reason for God to tell Daniel not to eat the king's food. He was better off physically as well as spiritually because he obeyed God. And look at all the extra, unexpected blessings God gave Daniel for being obedient (see Daniel 1:17). Do you think that you could also experience God's unexpected blessing if you dared to obey him?

5. Decide whether to emulate (parrot) or avoid the choices and consequences endured by the biblical character portrayed.

Let your congregation have a good look at the benefits of the God-honoring choices. Allow them to gaze on the ripple effect that those decisions had on their family, friends, and community and then bring them to the point of decision. Exhort your congregation to learn from the mistakes and successes of the heroes of Scripture.

- What is holding you back from making a God-honoring decision today?
- What are the pressures you face to imitate/reject the decision of the biblical character?
- How will your life be changed by your choice? What will happen to *your* story?
- How would the stories of *others* (e.g., your family, friends, church community) respond to and be affected by your decision to imitate the biblical character?

> Daniel made a God-honoring decision in spite of the lure of conformity and security. That decision released God's blessing on himself and those around him. What will you do in the similar situation that you are facing?

6. Alter behavior in accordance with the decision.

As a caring pastor, you know many of the issues that people in your congregation are struggling with. Give them specific examples of what the application of this passage might look like in their lives. Concretely outline how their actions might be different as a result of their choice. Challenge them to implement the lessons from this text into their lives immediately and to tell someone about their decision to do so.

- You won't quote a false early delivery date in order to make a sale. However, you will work to remove the red tape to reduce the shipping time.
- When the captain of the football team says he'll invite you to the party after the game if you will allow him to look at your paper during tomorrow's math exam, you will refuse to cheat. Instead, you will offer to help him study for the exam tonight.

In *The Healing Power of Stories*, Daniel Taylor says that "the stories we live by sometimes fall apart. They no longer adequately explain our experience or give us enough reason to get up in the morning. . . . In such cases we need to heal our broken stories. The best cure for a broken story is another story."[2] Daniel Taylor is right, but the stories that heal best are the stories that God gave us: Bible stories. Healthy lives are the harvest of godly choices. Story shaping can bring healing as people learn and implement God-honoring decision making.

Third-Person Preaching

This narrative genre-appropriate sermon form is as simple as it is neglected. In a third-person sermon, like the original biblical narratives, the preacher assumes the role of an omniscient narrator and weaves the events of history into a literary tapestry that communicates a theological point to a contemporary audience. This homiletical form can communicate the big idea of a narrative passage with great power and precision. But will only do so for those preachers who appreciate the significant role narrators occupy in storytelling.

The most common mistake that third-person preachers make is to simply "rerun" or retell the original narrative. For reasons more thoroughly discussed earlier, this is a significant misstep. The biblical story was inspired to be the best possible story to communicate its truth to the original audience. But those people are now dead, and you are preaching to people with a very different culture, history, and worldview than the original hearers of this narrative. You can only preserve the story's original meaning if you change its structure. Adapt it for its new context. How can you do this?

Like the original narrator, you must select the perspective from which to tell your story. What slant will you give to your story? From what perspective will it be told? Photographers are required to make the same decision. Deciding on the subject of a photograph is only the first of many choices that an artist using a lens must make. If it is a portrait shot and the goal is to make the subject look important, the camera may be angled from below. This makes the person look taller and more powerful. If the goal is to minimize the subject, the choice is made to take the shot from above. If the photographer wants to make a person look evil, they will shoot an unflattering expression under harsh lights, with sharp focus and black and white film. A glamour photograph will pull back to a respectable distance and shoot the most flattering angle when the subject has fresh makeup on, using soft lighting and a soft focus lens.

The artistic decisions made by the person behind the lens have a significant influence on how people ultimately respond to the subject of the photograph. Narrators wield a similar influence over their stories. The artistic decisions of the narrator determine how the people will respond to the idea presented within the story. The biblical narrator made the appropriate choices for the ancient audience, and you must make the appropriate choices for your contemporary congregation.

As the narrator of your story, you become omniscient. You know everything that is happening and what every character is thinking and feeling at every moment. A good narrator tells their audience everything they need to know, when they need to know it. Your listeners expect you to give them all the relevant information and insight needed for them to make sense out of the story. This makes it easy to insert the relevant historical and cultural information. Just be careful that you do not bury the tension of the story under the weight of unnecessary data.

Writing a third-person sermon is similar to that of creating a first-person sermon. Start stage 2 of the sermon preparation process by drawing a mono-mythic cycle on a blank piece of paper. At the very bottom of the circle, mark the unexpected twist of the biblical story. What is the conflict — where is the tension — of this story? Making sure that the tension and the twist of the original story are maintained. Ask yourself, "What scenes and information are needed for me to lead my listeners from summer down to winter and back?" Mark out those scenes on your mono-mythic cycle and use the Scene Development Chart to flesh them out.

An advantage of third-person preaching is the latitude it provides you with application. With third-person sermons you can walk into the world of your listeners. Your perspective is not as limited as with a first-person sermon. While you do not want to take this too far — or you will turn a narrative sermon into a didactic polemic — there is more elasticity with a third-person than with a first-person sermon. It is easier to make contemporary observations and application with a third-person sermon.

One of the disadvantages of this sermon form, however, is its ability to communicate emotion. The relative objectivity displayed by a narrator does not allow you to communicate the emotional intensity of an eyewitness. There is a big difference between hearing Dan Rather talk about a war in the Middle East and having a soldier who grew up next door to you relate how she fought for her life in hand-to-hand urban warfare. No sermon form can communicate raw emotion as intensely as a first-person sermon.

Counseling Sermons

Another arrow for your homiletical quiver is the counseling sermon. A counseling sermon uses the drama of an actual counseling situation as the vehicle to present the truth of a biblical passage. By observing how the truth of Scripture was concretely applied to strangers, your listeners will learn how and why it applies to them. Let me show you what I mean. Here is a summary of a third-person sermon I have preached.

It's hot today, isn't it?! Days like today remind me of a hot Saturday some years ago when I lived in a different city. It was so hot that day that I spent most of the morning puttering around in the garage hoping that my wife, Nola, would not find me and ask me to go outside and do chores in the hot sun. My fears were realized when she asked me to go and cut the grass. The lawn seemed fine to me, but Nola was determined that it should receive a trim in preparation for the guests who were coming over for lunch on Sunday.

When it was obvious I was not going to win this discussion, I fired up the hot lawnmower and started cutting the front lawn. While spending an unusually long time cutting under a shade tree, I noticed a couple on the sidewalk walking toward our home. I knew them. Not only did they attend the church I pastored, but I was also doing their premarital counseling. I will call them Bob and Mary.

As they paused by the tree, I shut off the lawnmower (it was the polite thing to do) and began chatting with them.

"How are things going?" I asked.

"Not too good," Bob confessed. "We have spent the last few days apartment hunting and don't know what to do. It is not that we can't find a suitable place, we found several that would do just fine. There is adequate housing available. We just can't afford any of it. We have worked through that budget sheet you gave us a thousand times and cannot make the numbers work. I even showed them to a financial advisor. He said that we could make it on our income if we did not give so much to the church. In his opinion, giving 10 percent of one's income to God is excessive. Who says we have to tithe anyway? Where did the whole concept come from?"

At this point, I thought that I had a good enough reason to escape the heat. If we were going to talk, we may as well do so where it was cooler. One of the advantages of having a wife who grew up in the South is that she knew how to make genuine sweet tea. Not that fake powdered stuff. We came in the back door and found a jug of tea steaming on the counter. I poured it into tall glasses filled with ice and enjoyed the sound of the ice cracking, and we made our way into the living room. I took some Bibles off the bookshelf and we all turned to Malachi 3. You may want to turn along to that very same passage. After we turned I read verses 6–8.

> "I the LORD do not change. So you, O descendants of Jacob, are not destroyed. Ever since the time of your forefathers you have turned away from my decrees and have not kept them. Return to me, and I will return to you," says the LORD Almighty.
> "But you ask, 'How are we to return?'
> "Will a man rob God? Yet you rob me.
> "But you ask, 'How do we rob you?'
> "In tithes and offerings."

"I know that we should give offerings," Bob interrupted. "I have grown up with offering plates. But who said we had to give 10 percent? Why not 5 percent? I think we could make our budget work if we gave somewhere between 2–3 percent!"

"Good question," I responded. "Malachi did not invent tithing. The concept of tithing is old. It predates the Old Testament law—it is as ancient as the book of Genesis." (I then spoke to them about the example Abraham set when he gave 10 percent to the priest Melchizedek in Genesis 14.)

"The concept of tithing didn't end there. God extended its relevance by entrenching it in the law he gave his people." (I then spoke about the significance of tithing in the period of the Old Testament law.)

"Yes," Mary said. "That is interesting, but wasn't the law set aside with the coming of Christ? Are we not free to give whatever we want today?"

"Things did change dramatically with the coming of Christ," I responded. "But it is interesting how Jesus specifically addressed the issue of tithing. In Matthew 23:23 Jesus said, 'Woe to you, teachers of the law and Pharisees, you hypocrites! You give a tenth of your spices—mint, dill and cummin. But you have neglected the more important matters of the law—justice, mercy and faithfulness. You should have practiced the latter, without neglecting the former.'" (I then related this to Paul's teaching on giving to the Corinthians, showing how the apostle's teaching on tithing was not antithetical to the teaching of the Old Testament.)

"Malachi is telling the people of God that the tithe belongs to God. When we place it in the offering plate, we are acknowledging his pre-eminence over all we are and everything we have. Giving the tithe is non-negotiable. To spend God's money on us is thievery. This explains why in Malachi 3:9–10a the prophet said: 'You are under a curse—the whole nation of you—because you are robbing me. Bring the whole tithe into the storehouse, that there may be food in my house.'

"When we refuse to tithe, we harm ourselves and starve the work of God in the world. You have seen this in everyday life. People who are tightfisted toward God have shriveled hearts. Churches populated by people that don't tithe have shriveled ministries. You don't want this to be true of your life."

"I can see that is true," they said almost in unison, "but if we start tithing, we will be bankrupt in just a few months! It is impossible!"

"Look at verses 10b—12," I said:

> "Test me in this," says the LORD Almighty, "and see if I will not throw open the floodgates of heaven and pour out so much blessing that you will not have room enough for it. I will prevent pests from devouring your crops, and the vines in your fields will not cast their fruit," says the LORD Almighty. "Then all the nations will call you blessed, for yours will be a delightful land," says the LORD Almighty.

"God is inviting us here to take him with the most sensitive part of our anatomy—our wallet. If we are willing to trust him fiscally, he will provide for us monetarily. God will protect us from financial losses that would have come our way and will give us blessing we would have missed. We are far better off trusting our sovereign God than stealing his money.

"God honors those who honor him. This is a basic principle of Scripture. The question we have to answer as we make up our budget is who comes first: him or me?"

Bob and Mary finished a second glass of iced tea. Before they continued their walk, they promised to talk about the passage some more and make a decision. The next morning at church they asked the treasurer for offering envelopes and began a lifetime practice of tithing. They returned from their brief honeymoon to a small apartment, and they have always paid their rent on time.

It has been over fifteen years since Bob, Mary, and I shared a hot Saturday afternoon together looking at what the Bible says about tithing. I can tell you that if it were possible for Mary and Bob to be here this morning, they would tell you that God has protected and provided for them in ways that they could never have imagined. They have honored God, and God has honored them. When you are wrestling with your monthly budget and trying to make ends meet, will you do what they did? Will you consider the words of Malachi? Don't steal God's money. Take his blessing instead.

Consider the many advantages of preaching a counseling sermon. The relevance of your message becomes immediately apparent. Like the narratives themselves, counseling sermons deal with the concrete significant issues of life. Unlike many other sermon forms, however, counseling sermons allow you to deal with the most sensitive issues in a nonconfrontational tone that does not raise the defenses of a potentially resistant audience. Its conversational format helps put people at ease. Counseling sermons also excel at dealing with objections. They allow you to naturally raise and reply to the questions that your audience would ask if they were having coffee with you.

Counseling sermons also have a natural ability to persuade. Why? Because it is human nature to discount what is told to us directly and to believe wholeheartedly what we overhear. If the chairperson of your church board tells you that you preached a good sermon, you would say "thank you" and wonder how authentic his compliment was. It could be politeness or politics. If a few days later, however, you overhear the chairperson telling an office coworker in a restaurant, "This past Sunday my pastor preached the best sermon I have ever heard. He is fantastic!" you are more likely to believe him. We tend to believe what we overhear. Counseling sermons are truth overheard.

A word of caution, however. Be careful to disguise the identities and get permission from all of the people featured in your sermon. You do not want to create unwanted publicity for those involved or create any confidentiality issues. In addition, if you invent a counseling scenario for the sake of a message, do not pretend that it actually occurred. A lie is a poor foundation for a sermon. Above all else, we are to be men and women of integrity. If an event happened, you can say so. If the event is fictitious, you must make this clear.

Parabolic Preaching

Another narrative homiletical option available is parabolic preaching. A parabolic mirror is not a typical mirror. This mirror's unique concave shape allows it to organize and focus the light at its focal point with amazing efficiency. This focused light penetrates darkness so effectively that parabolic mirrors are used regularly in headlights and searchlights.

A parabolic story is not a typical story. Like the parables of Jesus, these are contemporary stories sculpted to collect and then project the idea of a biblical text with maximum effect into the minds of the listeners. As Jesus did with his parables, you can create a fictitious story to communicate a genuine theological idea. His stories brought spiritual illumination to the lives of others. Yours can as well.

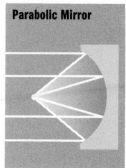

Parabolic Mirror

The preparation of a parabolic sermon begins after all of the hard work of stage 1, that is, when you have arrived at a clear understanding of the big idea of the biblical passage. Only when you are clear what the biblical narrative is saying can you begin to design a contemporary story that does exactly what the original did. The content can be different, but the idea and impact must be the same. Let me illustrate this by summarizing a sermon on Luke 4:31–44 in which I used a parabolic story.

This morning I would like to tell you a story that is entirely fictitious, and yet every word of it is true.

David and Doreen Falstaff were married during seminary and graduated with a passion to preach the Scriptures and win souls for Jesus Christ. They were prepared to do everything in their power to bring men and women to him. As the winner of the "senior preacher" award, David was offered a number of lucrative ministry positions. Rather than take them, however, the Falstaffs chose to do something more dramatic with their gifts and passions. They decided to plant a church in inner-city Detroit. Why Detroit? "Because statistically," they would reply, "churches are needed as desperately there as any other place in America. God has called us to preach the word and evangelize the lost."

They arrived in Detroit the fall after graduation to begin their preaching-evangelistic work and caught a break almost immediately. A local executive gave them a small white house right downtown situated on a huge lot—almost an entire city block! Everything except the house was a burned-out graffiti-stained mess, but it was a place to begin. The donor got a huge tax write-off from the mission, and David and Doreen got a mission headquarters. They set up chairs and put an old donated pulpit at the front of the largest room. Before going to bed, he ran his hands over that wobbly pulpit thinking about the many sermons he would preach from that humble wooden structure. "Today we begin our mission: a sufficient word for a spiritually needy world," he said to Doreen with great excitement.

The excitement did not last long. Before arriving, the Falstaffs had managed to raise only the minimum level of financial support. Now they wondered who had thought anyone could survive on so little. Things were tight. Too tight. Some days they were hungry. As the snow began to fall, their spirits plunged with the temperature. This was tough work!

It was bad enough to be living in poverty, but to do so in order to minister to a community that was not very interested was almost more than they could bear. Only a handful of people showed up to hear David's carefully constructed messages. He discovered how tough it was to preach to only fourteen people! Even fewer were interested in committing their lives to Christ. Discouragement began to settle into the pit of their souls. Thoughts of quitting began to dance in their heads.

One day Doreen suggested that she use her nursing training to help draw people into the church. David agreed. The results were astonishing. The prostitutes, drug users, and other noninsureds began to show up in droves. Doreen was soon run off her feet in the face of all the need! The few supplies that they had quickly ran out, and David began spending an increasing amount of time fund-raising for this burgeoning ministry. David had a flair for administration and began to use it with the clinic. They began using medical volunteers and hiring various medical staff as David managed to get the money. Some of the funds came from the city, most from Christian individuals and ministries. The demands on their time were overwhelming.

David continued to preach, of course, but it was not the central focus of his ministry. As the years ticked by and the clinic continued to grow, David and Doreen talked about whether they should refocus their ministry. They were now in the middle years of ministry. If they were going to make a change, this was the time. Then Bill Clinton arrived.

Bill Clinton was campaigning for the White House and looking for local volunteers to champion. The Falstaffs were perfect—an energetic couple devoting themselves to helping the physical needs of others in the heart of one of the toughest cities of the nation. This was the kind of local initiative that Bill wanted to encourage! And be photographed next to. Vote for him and federal funds would be made available to construct a much larger medical facility. As things worked out, Clinton was elected and huge amounts of money arrived. The burned-out city block was cleared and a huge state-of-the-art facility was constructed. It was big, shiny, and busy. At the very center stood the old white wooden house with its wobbly pulpit—built into the heart of the facility. A memory of the early years.

David and Doreen now worked harder than ever and accomplished a great deal. As the years passed, various organizations kept honoring the Falstaffs for their contributions. Finally, last September David and Doreen retired. They had given their lives to this hospital. They were tired, and the thought of one more Detroit winter was more than they could bear.

They decided to end their career at the hospital the way that they had started all those years ago. They would hold a service in the old wooden house. As David cracked open his Bible and felt the familiar wobble of the pulpit, he realized that only a dozen people showed up. As they headed the Winnebago south toward Arizona, David turned to Doreen and asked the million-dollar question. "Honey, were we successful? I know we did a great deal, but did we do what God had called us to do? We did a lot of good, but did we do the best? Did we give the sufficient word to a spiritually needy world?"

The question that the Falstaffs asked themselves at the end of their ministry was the same one that Jesus asked at the beginning of his. In

Luke 4 Jesus began his ministry. In these early days, the people were "amazed at his teaching." He was a preacher par excellence! Yet we discover a shift of ministry emphasis occurring in this chapter—a shift away from preaching that started at Satan's initiative. In verses 34 and 41, evil spirits generated large crowds for Jesus by announcing his identity, crowds that came for healing. "News about him spread throughout the surrounding area" (v. 37) so that "when the sun was setting, the people brought to Jesus all who had various kinds of sickness, and laying his hands on each one, he healed them" (v. 40).

The demands for healing were increasing exponentially. To meet this increasing demand, Jesus was forced to dedicate an increasing amount of time and energy. The demands reached such a level that Luke tells us in Luke 4:42 that "at daybreak Jesus went out to a solitary place. The people were looking for him and when they came to where he was, they tried to keep him from leaving them." The cry of the people was for Jesus to shift his ministry priorities—to preach less and to heal more.

To stop Jesus from reaching peak ministry effectiveness, Satan had sent his evil spirits to generate ministry opportunity for Jesus. Legitimate ministry opportunity. Good ministry that would keep Jesus so busy that he would not have time for the best ministry that his Father wanted him to have. The temptation to exchange the best for good is so subtle and strong that Jesus needed to get up extra early and spend additional time in prayer before he could reassert his ministry priorities to the clamoring crowds. "I must preach the good news of the kingdom of God to the other towns also, because that is why I was sent" (Luke 4:43). Jesus would continue to heal people. But he would not allow healing to deflect him from his primary purpose. First and foremost, Jesus knew he was to be a preacher! Jesus always kept first things first. He did not let himself get sidetracked by the second best.

The Falstaffs allowed the primary passion and purpose of their ministry to be supplanted. They did good things and had a wonderful ministry. But they discovered at the end of their ministry that they allowed opportunity to deflect them from their principal calling. Don't let Satan do the same in your life. Don't let him marginalize your ministry effectiveness. Refuse to exchange the best for the good.

In parabolic preaching, we are blatantly tearing a page out of Jesus' preaching manual. We create a theological story that will concretize and contemporize the big idea of a biblical passage. Your story can be very different from the biblical account, but be sure to keep three things in mind.

- Make clear to your listeners before you begin whether your story is true to history or true to life.

- Make sure that your story has the same big idea that the biblical text does. I am advocating innovation, not fancification.
- Take some time to show and explain to your listeners the biblical story that your parable is based on. This is an expository sermon, not story time.

Refurbished Stories

If you would prefer to preach a narrative sermon that follows the detail of the biblical narrative somewhat closer, you can refurbish one. A refurbished house is the original house modernized. It resembles the old one but is filled with modern accoutrements that the original occupants would never have recognized. A refurbished sermon is similar. In it the essential structure of the original story is preserved but the details allow a modern audience to feel more comfortable and identify more easily.

I have used the refurbished story method successfully with the parable of the prodigal son. All the characters of Jesus are preserved and the basic plot line is unchanged. But everything else is different. It begins something like this:

> This morning I would like to tell you a story, a story that takes place in a mythical town called Rolling Hills. Rolling Hills is a small burg of about 1,100 people located somewhere out in the Midwest. Before it was bypassed by the new interstate, Rolling Hills could have been considered locally significant. Not any more.
>
> It does have some significant people living there, however. One of those is Frank. Frank owns the Mobil station in Rolling Hills and is the kindest, most generous man you will ever meet. If you get to the bank too late on a Friday night, stop by Frank's. He will let you sign your check and give you the cash. If your wife lands a new job but needs the car fixed in order to get to work, go see Frank. He will fix it now and let you pay him back as the money begins to come in. Frank is in a class of his own.
>
> Frank has two sons, Mark and Steve. Those boys are as different as night and day. Frank loves them both, don't get me wrong. He loves them both so much that he went out and bought the local GM dealership. He built the small showroom right next door to the station. With so many young people leaving town after high school, this was Frank's way of showing his boys he loved them and wanted them to build a life with him right there in Rolling Hills. Mark, the older boy, seemed to really respond. After high school he went to the local community college and took a few management training courses. Now he works at the dealership full-time. Mark is a clean-cut, obey-the-rules, mind-your-manners kind of kid. He looks like a good son.

Steve, on the other hand . . . he is different from his brother. A real embarrassment to his father. Steve is not interested in helping out at the station or building a career at the dealership. He just complains all the time that nothing exciting has ever happened or will ever happen in Rolling Hills. He doesn't even try to hide his contempt for his town or a father who decided to live there. What interests him is New York— now that is where the action is! All he thinks about is how he can escape from Rolling Hills and do interesting things with interesting people. Two weeks before the date of his high school graduation, he made his move.

"Dad," he said one evening after "hoovering" three helpings from his dinner plate, "Dad, I feel like I need to stretch my wings. I am an adult now—almost a high school graduate! And I want to go where I can really make it big. And there is nothing bigger than New York City! I have made up my mind. The day after I graduate I am heading off to New York City to seek my fortune. All I need is money to get a fresh start. What I want is my inheritance—early. You are going to give it to me one day, why not now? I have big plans for all that cash!"

I am sure you can tell what is happening here. Frank, in spite of the deep humiliation, gives Steve his inheritance. Steve goes off to New York City and wastes the inheritance. Soon Steve is hungrier than he has ever been in his life. And when he arrives home, Frank is waiting to welcome him home. I ended the story this way.

The story I have told you this morning is not original. I plagiarized it. It was first told 2,000 years ago by Jesus Christ. He didn't tell that story just to entertain us, but to tell us about God. Frank? He represents God, our heavenly Father—a heavenly Father who loves us more than we can ever imagine or deserve. Steve? That is us: willful, ungrateful, and unworthy of his love. But God knows that. He knows us just as well as Frank knew Steve. And yet, even now, God is standing, looking out of his bedroom window, looking to see if you want to come home.

All we have to do is come home to him. To acknowledge that we have sinned. God is waiting for you as Frank was for Steve. Waiting to forgive. Waiting to wrap his arms around you and say welcome home! To say I missed you, child. All is forgiven. Will you come?

Don't overlook refurbished stories as you plan your preaching schedule. While caution is obviously required to ensure that the integrity of the original narrative is preserved, refurbishing a biblical story is like adding new music to familiar lyrics. You allow these old, old stories to sing to a brand-new generation.

Morphing in the Pulpit

Sermon morphing occurs when you change your homiletical form part way through your sermon. Just because you began your sermon in a "traditional" mode doesn't mean that you have to stick with that style all the way to your conclusion. Everything changes. Why not your sermon form?

Suppose, for example, that you were preaching a fairly traditional sermon on Abraham being called by God from the Ur of the Chaldees. And you quoted the famous verse: "The LORD had said to Abram, 'Leave your country, your people and your father's household and go to the land I will show you'" (Gen. 12:1).

> God asked Abram to leave Ur, the most sophisticated urban environment of his day to go who knows where. Can you imagine how the dinner table conversation went that evening?
>
> "Sarai, honey, this is wonderful lamb. Really good. I can't tell you how much I have appreciated your cooking lately. By the way, we are moving."
>
> "Moving? Who says so? I like it here! This is where family is and Mother is getting on in years. Besides, the shopping is excellent and I just ordered new drapes."
>
> "I know, honey, I like it here too, but God told me to move."
>
> "He did? Well, where exactly did he say we were moving to?"
>
> "He didn't. He just said to move. I think he intends to tell us on the way."
>
> "On the way? Who ever heard of starting a journey without knowing the destination? What direction are you going to start walking? How many provisions are you going to need? What should we sell and what should we keep? Do you want to know what I think, Abe? I think that you and God need to go back, have another conversation, and get some of these details worked out. I ain't going nowhere until I know what to pack!"

I don't think we appreciate the enormity of what God was asking Abram to do. Nor do we understand the faith that both Abram and Sarai demonstrated as they began to live a life of total faith.

By morphing into and out of a first-person genre, you not only increase the interest of your congregation, but you are able to give emotional insight on a biblical passage that could not be done as effectively if you gave a detached description of the event. Besides, if you do it well, most of the congregation will not even realize that you morphed from one genre to another. They will just notice that you got a lot more interesting.

The narrative sermon forms that I have outlined in this chapter are representative and suggestive. They are not definitive. You are welcome to experiment and invent. Just make sure of two things. First, the big idea of the biblical text must be clearly communicated. Second, make sure that the four characteristics of narratives — tension, concretism, emotion, and literary artistry — are present in your homiletical forms. With these two cautions in mind have fun! Be creative! Communicate God's stories with maximum impact.

To be a great preacher you need the head of a scholar, the heart of a poet, and the knees of a prayer warrior. Head, heart, and soul. It takes all that you have. This is why a call to preach is the most intellectually, creatively, and spiritually demanding calling there is. But when you give yourself to it, when you commit your life to the faithful, relevant exposition of God's Word, you will see lives transformed into the image of Christ. And this will further motivate you to give your utmost for his highest.

NOTES FOR CHAPTER EIGHT

1. Eugene L. Lowry, *The Homiletical Plot* (Atlanta: John Knox, 1980).
2. Daniel Taylor, *The Healing Power of Stories* (New York: Doubleday, 1996), 113.

EXAMPLES OF NARRATIVE PREACHING

Samson: The Strong Weak Man

JUDGES 13 – 16

J. KENT EDWARDS

Hello. My name is Samson. I can tell from the looks on some of your faces that you recognize my name. I'm not surprised. After all, when I lived here on earth, I was the most famous man in the world. Everyone knew the name of Samson. And they spoke it with respect. They had to. I was the strongest man who ever lived. If I were alive today, you'd not only admit me into your Olympics, but you'd have to set up a special category for me. Because I'm the strongest man of all time—bar none. What? You think I'm exaggerating? Overstating my case a little bit? Well, let me tell you the facts and you decide whether my claim is true or not.

As a young man, I fell in love with the wrong kind of woman. She was not of my people. The woman was a Philistine who lived in Timnah. My parents were disappointed with my decision to marry her, but what could they do? In order to make arrangements for the wedding I had to make the journey to Timnah. The terrain for my journey was dangerous; rocks and bushes were scattered across the hilly terrain—perfect hiding spaces for bandits! Even though I kept scanning the horizon looking for danger, I was not prepared for what happened. Out of the corner of my eye I caught sight of something worse than a bandit—I saw a golden blur flying out from behind some boulders towards me. It was a lion!

Not the kind of lion that you're thinking about. Not the caged excuse for an animal that you're familiar with. The kind that sit around all day and eat at 10 a.m. and 4 p.m. when someone throws them dead meat. Not that kind of a lion. I mean a *real* lion. A young lion. One who's learned to think on his feet and to live by its wits. A lion whose body has been honed by constant action and constant killing. One with jaws so strong it can snap the bones of an animal just like that (*snap fingers*).

As I'm walking along the road to Timnah thinking about my wedding night and the plans that have to precede it, this lion suddenly lets loose a roar and launches itself through the air toward me. I just caught a glimpse of it out of the corner of my eye before it reached me. Its roar was intended to paralyze its prey with fear. The speed and weight of its body were intended to knock its prey off its feet. Its jaws were intended to rip its prey to pieces.

What would you have done at that instant. Freeze? Cry for your mother? Make a mess? Do you know what I did? Without a moment's hesitation (because there wasn't a moment to spare), as the lion leapt toward me ready for the kill, I bent down and grabbed it from underneath. And as it passed over me I grabbed hold of each end and began pulling. You could hear the cracking of bones and the ripping of sinew and then, suddenly, there was the lion at the side of the road. In two parts. I stood in awe of my own handiwork. And when the carcass stopped twitching, I knew that I really was the strongest man who ever lived.

Still doubt my claim? Still not sure I was the strongest man who ever lived? Let me give you another example, and you make up your own mind. When I lived here on earth, the Philistines were Israel's number one enemy. They brutalized and oppressed my people. With their advantage in weaponry and training, these pagan warriors descended on Israelite homes and fields almost at will. They decimated our flocks and crops and stole whatever they wanted. No Israelite could stop them. No one could frustrate their evil purposes. No one but me. Only Samson. They knew that I was only one. The only one who stood between them and their quest for total domination of Israel. Only Samson could resist them.

So one day the Philistine commanders came to the elders of an Israelite town and said to them: "Give us Samson or we will wreak our vengeance on you."

So a delegation of 3,000 Israelite men came to me and said, "Samson, we don't want to turn you over to the Philistines—we know that they intend to kill you, but what choice do we have? If we do not hand you over to them, they will kill us all!"

I said to them: "Guys, it's OK. The Philistines don't know who they're messing with. What I want you to do is to tie me up with two new ropes."

Not the kind of ropes that you are thinking of! Not binder twine. Not that skimpy yellow stuff you use around the house. I'm talking about rope, real hemp rope. The rope as thick as your arm that is used at seaports to tie up the ocean-going vessels.

I told my countrymen: "Tie me up with two new ropes and hand me over to the Philistines."

"But," they stammered, "you won't have a chance. They will kill you for sure!"

"Don't argue," I said, "just do it, OK? Hand me over to them."

And they did. They tied me with two new ropes. A little more snug than perhaps they needed to, but they did what I asked. And then they placed me at the end of a field—with the Philistine hoard, an army of 15,000 warriors, waiting for me at the other end of the field. After putting me in place, my countrymen left me alone—melting away into the countryside so they wouldn't get in the Philistines' way.

As I stood there under the hot sun, abandoned and alone at my end of the field, the Philistines couldn't believe their good luck! All they had done was apply a little pressure to the townsfolk and my fellow Israelites had rolled over on me at the first opportunity! This was too easy! The Philistines were sure that this was their lucky day. Standing defenseless at the far end of the field was me, their only Israelite opposition!

At this point the Philistine soldiers started running. They ran because they knew what was at stake. They knew that the person who got me first would receive a prize. They knew that the man who thrust his sword into my heart and held my severed head aloft would be long remembered in Philistine lore. And each man wanted that honor. Each one wanted to be remembered as the champion who slew Samson! To him would go the spoils of war! And so they started running down the field toward me.

As they came I just stood there—standing bound and helpless before them. As the 15,000 men ran toward me I could feel the ground shake. They kept coming faster and faster, their war cry filling the air. When they were about two-thirds of the way down the field, I took my stance. As I began to press against the ropes, I could feel the warmth of the Spirit of the Lord coming upon me and coursing through my veins. And those new hemp ropes? They became like charred flax. I snapped them as if they were burnt thread.

When the Philistines leading the charge saw what I had done to those ropes, they were not quite as eager to claim their glory. They began to express "a new willingness" to share their anticipated glory—they wanted to let others go first. The problem was, however, that the soldiers further back had not seen the ropes snap, and they weren't stopping. The ones at the back were still running as fast as they could. Running, pushing the ones in front toward me.

I looked around to see if there was anything I could use as a weapon. Nothing! Only the Philistines had weapons. It was always that way when we fought the Philistines. What an insult! How could I fight without a weapon? There was nothing around except a dead donkey. As I kicked at the donkey carcass in frustration, I realized that it was relatively fresh. The teeth were still in the jawbone! I picked it up. I had what I needed. I took my stance.

Now the Philistines at the front of the crowd *really* wanted to let the ones farther back go first! But they didn't have any choice. They couldn't stop. And I didn't run. Instead, I began to walk toward them. The donkey's jawbone became my sword. As the soldiers enveloped me I went wild. Spinning one way and then another. Ducking low one moment and swinging high the next. As I danced my deadly dance, Philistines began to scream. And die. The Philistine army was thrown into such confusion that they began to trample over each other in a desperate attempt to escape. Their losses were enormous. When the dust finally settled that afternoon, a thousand Philistines lay dead, and the others were running for their lives. 15,000 men to 1! Not bad, eh?

Still not sure that I was the strongest man that ever lived? Still need more evidence? OK. One more story. One day I found myself in Gaza. I guess I was bored. Gaza, a Philistine city on the seacoast, intrigued me. I had not spent much time on the seacoast. I disguised myself well and began to mingle with the people who filled the busy streets. As I began to relax in my supposed anonymity I saw a lady of the evening advertising her wares. And I liked what I saw. I knew that it was wrong, but I paid money to spend time with her. In the middle of the night, when I was finished, I began to make my leave. It was then that I realized that I had not disguised my appearance as well as I thought.

Sometime during the past few hours, the Philistines had identified me. Gaza's city fathers had realized that they had Samson in town and sent for reinforcements in order to capture or kill me. Their plan was clear. They intended to delay my departure long enough for help to arrive. It was relatively easy for them to do this. Gaza, like all Philistine cities, was surrounded by large walls. Walls higher than you could throw a stone over and wide enough to ride a chariot on. These were huge stone walls built with the strength they needed to keep enemies out.

Philistine cities had only one defensive weakness—their gate. Because people needed to go in and out of the city to work their farms and conduct their trades, every city had a huge gate. The gate was considered the strength of the city. And this one was strong all right. It went from the ground up to the top of those walls. It was made of solid hardwood, 6 feet thick, and was mounted with solid bronze hinges to huge posts buried 10 to 15 feet in the ground. As if that were not enough, the entire structure was reinforced with bronze bars. It was immense! When they closed their gate, no one could go in or out of the city. If they closed it when I was still inside, I would have no way out. I would be trapped, and the Philistines knew it.

I began to suspect something was up in the middle of the night as I began to make my way back home. As I walked through the streets I saw shuttered windows and heard people whispering: "We have him! At long last Samson is ours!" As I turned the corner and saw those massive gates shut and locked, the plan of the city fathers became obvious. They had me trapped like a lion in a cage. Or at least they thought so. I don't know what you might have done in that situation. Try to hide, maybe? Try to pick the lock? Scale the wall? That wasn't my style. That's not Samson.

I didn't quiver in fear. I walked straight and boldly right through town until I came to the main gate. I stood in the courtyard for a moment and then turned around to make sure everyone knew who I was. Then I walked up to those gates. I spat on my hands, bent down, and grabbed hold of a reinforcing bar. Boy, I was glad they put it there! It made a great handle. Then I began to pull. Harder and harder. As I pulled, I began to feel the inner warmth of God's Spirit as he began to course through my body. As I pulled harder and harder the supernatural heat spiked with intensity. I began to hear creaks, and then groaning, and finally the snapping of timbers as the gate came wrenching right out of the ground.

A lesser man might have just dropped it on the ground and walked away. But I decided that would not be humiliating enough. So I lifted the gate up on my shoulder and carried it to the top of that hill twenty-eight miles away and dropped it there. They could go get a team of horses and pull it back if they wanted to, but it wasn't good enough for me just to escape from that town. I wanted to embarrass them. That was the strength of their city and I stole it. I am the strongest man that ever lived. No question. No argument.

What bothers me, however, is that when people like you remember me, they think of me only as a strong man. Not a great man. And I could have been great. I should have been great.

Even my birth was special. It was announced by the angel of the Lord. By God himself! I was his gift to a barren couple and to a nation in distress. The angel told my parents: "You are going to have a son—a son with a mission in life. The purpose of his life is to set Israel free from the Philistines." My mission was clear; my path of life had been laid out in front of me.

Then the angel of the Lord went on: "The only thing you need to know, the only thing that he must remember, is that he must be raised as and live like a Nazirite." What makes a Nazirite so special? Three simple rules. My mom told them to me over and over again when I was growing up. Parents are like that sometimes.

- "Don't forget, you can't touch any unclean thing, Samson. Don't go near there. You can't touch any carcasses, any dead animals." "I know, Mom. I know. You've told me a million times."
- "Samson, don't go over there. That's where all that drink is served. All that fermented stuff. No fermented drink is to touch your lips. You are a Nazirite. Don't go close." "Mom . . . you get too uptight."
- My dad said to me, "Samson, remember, never cut your hair." Not many fathers have said that to their sons through the centuries. "I know, Dad. That's the visible sign that I'm a Nazirite and everyone will recognize who I am because it's so unusual." Parents can be such a pain sometimes!

My problem was not lack of knowledge. It was lack of obedience. I remember the day I headed back to Timnah. This was my second visit. As you recall, I had gone to Timnah once before—to make the arrangements for my upcoming wedding. But now the time of the wedding celebration was approaching. It was time to get married. As I was walking back down that same road to Timnah, I couldn't believe how hot it was. I don't know what it is like around here, but where I grew up, it is hot. Where I lived, the sun not only beats down on you, it also sucks the life right outta ya. I mean, I know I'm strong, but the sun . . . ahhh.

As I'm heading down the road, it is getting worse and worse and I don't know if I can go on. And I am starting to get light-headed. I need to eat! I am not sure if it was ego or curiosity, but when I came to the spot in the road where I ripped the lion in half, I walked over to take a look . . . and there was honey! Bees had made hives right there in the carcass! All I could see was foood! I didn't even think, I just plunged my hand into the heart of the hive and pulled out some honeycomb. I can tell you that nothing had ever tasted sweeter!

There I was eating the comb with honey dripping down my arms and all over my beard and in my mouth and I felt good. You know how when you finally get food, how wonderful that sugar rush is? You can feel the strength just coursing through your body again! And *ahhh* it felt so good getting that food in. Now I knew that I could make the rest of my journey.

And then I remembered . . . I remembered what my mother had said and what the angel of the Lord had said . . . that I wasn't to touch any unclean thing. And I realized that by doing this I had touched a carcass and I'd broken my vow. I waited and looked at the sky for lightning to come or God to swallow me with an earthquake or . . . but nothing happened. Hmm . . . maybe my parents were wrong. Nothing happened. Maybe sin isn't that serious.

I went on and arrived at Timnah and we threw a party. Boy, what a party it was! When you start celebrating with Philistines—these coarse, military people who loved hunting and killing—you really had to let it all out. You had to be as wild as they were. I can tell you that no wedding celebration was anything like this! Philistine wedding feasts go on for days. It was a wild and raucous time. And it cost me a fortune.

When you marry outside of your faith, you've got to be careful. When you are in a different environment, you want to be sure that you are culturally sensitive and appropriate. So I made sure I spent the money that I needed to for all the local breads and cheeses and meats . . . you just have to understand the culture.

Philistines, of course, are seriously into drinking. They let me know about all of the wines and beers that are appropriate for the occasion and I sprang for them. The party went on day after day and night after night. It was a marvelous celebration. Of course all the Philistine guys are checking me out. You know what that's like. They want to see if I am a real man, and I'm trying to prove that I'm one of the guys. And you know, I'm a man's man, and everyone else is drinking it down . . . what's one Philistine beer? Oh my goodness, that stuff tastes terrible!!! . . . And I suddenly realized . . . that was number two. I had broken the *second* Nazirite vow!

I looked around, wondering if God would hit me with a fire bolt. What would be the consequences of my sin? I didn't pause for quite as long this time. I wasn't quite as afraid, but still I wondered what God would do. And you know what he did? Nothing! Nothing at all! I began to think that maybe all this sin talk was overblown. After all, the first two vows were broken and nothing happened. Life just went on. Not with that woman, by the way. Things didn't work out. There's another story there. A lot of dead Philistines at the end of that story too. But . . . life went on. Without a serious girlfriend.

Then one day I thought I had met the answer to my prayers. I met a woman. Not just any old woman. I met *the* woman. Hah . . . she had black hair. She had olive skin. She had eyes that would just melt you. Boy, could she fill a dress. This was a woman! Her name was . . . *(pause for audience response . . . Delilah).* You know her! Actually, I'm not all that surprised you know of Delilah . . . she, she was amazing. She captured your imagination. She enthralled you. Her beauty, her wit, her charm . . . everything about her was ideal. . . . If you dreamt of the perfect woman, you would be dreaming of my Delilah. This was the perfect woman; she had everything a man could ever want. You couldn't imagine anything else. Except for one little thing . . . she was perfect except . . . she was a nag. She was easy on the eyes, but *she was a nag*!

When she got something under her skin, she just kept going and going and going until she got it. And she wanted to know the secret of my strength. "Samson," she says, "if you love me, we'll have an honest, transparent relationship. Tell me the secret of your strength." She fluttered her eyes. She tossed her hair. And I broke.

I told her, "If you just tie me up with some fresh thongs, then my strength will be gone." And she was happy and we had a wonderful evening. Then, in the middle of the night, suddenly she says to me, "Samson, the Philistines are here!" And I saw a bunch of Philistine soldiers halfway through the door. I got up and flexed my muscles and the thongs broke as if they were nothing. I charged the door and most of them got away. One didn't. They found him in the morning.

But Delilah was disappointed in me. "Samson, you haven't been entirely forthcoming with me." Women! I said, "Well, if you tie me with some new ropes that have never been used, that will do it."

"Oh well, I'm glad we've finally moved on in our relationship, Samson. Thank you." Later that night, "Samson, the Philistines are here!" Two new ropes—bang— they're gone like charred flax again. I didn't catch them that time. They were gone a bit faster this time. I figured they'd heard stories about the night before.

Delilah said, "Oh Samson, we have a trust issue here that just must be dealt with!"

So I gave her another line. "The secret of my strength really is my hair . . . if you braid it a certain way, the strength is gone. Trust me on this."

Then, in the middle of the night, once again, "Samson, the Philistines are here!" This time they just kind of peeked in the window. I was up and after them like no one's business, but they were gone.

Delilah said to me, "I cannot go forward with you if you cannot be honest."

"Look," I said, "just give it a rest. This doesn't involve you. This is personal. Please don't do this."

"Oh please, Samson, Samson. Don't you love me?" She kept whining. Oh man, that is just torture. Give me 15,000 soldiers any day. But this one pretty woman was driving me to distraction! She would *not* let up.

Finally, I told her about that one Nazirite vow I had not broken. I told her about how I was never to cut my hair. As I looked into her eyes, I was sure that

I could trust her. That night, I fell asleep with my head in her lap. The sleep of total trust.

But I was betrayed. As I slept, she had someone come and cut my hair and tie me up. Then she called, "Samson, the Philistines are here! Samson, the Philistines are here!" I got up as I had so many times before. I thought, "This is getting old, you know what I mean. We've done this sooo many times. Don't you guys ever learn?" The soldiers sent to get me had barely one eye against the window, just to take a quick look, before they ran for their lives.

I woke up, saw them peeking around the corner, and said, "Yeah, come get me, guys." And then I pushed against the rope. And then I pushed again. And again. I didn't know what was happening. I didn't know why it wouldn't break as before. And I pushed harder and harder. And the soldiers moved from the window to the door. And then they started inching a little bit closer, and a little bit closer. And finally they realized that my supernatural strength had left me. I began to lunge toward the door in a desperate attempt to escape. I took a couple of them down, but there were too many of them. More grabbed me, and more, and they held me. They pinned me.

And as I turned to look back at Delilah, I realized as I turned my head that I didn't feel my hair on the back of my neck. I realized that it was gone. And as I looked and cried out to Delilah, "Why?" I saw the soldiers pay her. She had sold me out. The last thing I saw was the knife of one of those soldiers as he plunged it first into one eye and then the next. The pain!!! I didn't know how I would stand it. The blood . . . the agony.

They laughed. They jeered. "The champion of Israel, we have him! Even if his strength comes back, he's blind, he's ours. He'll never be able to take us on again." They led me by the hand, knowing I couldn't resist, down into the bowels of a building. Down where they had a grinding wheel and they unhitched an ox and tied me to that wheel. They said, "Your job now is to grind grain to feed Philistine warriors."

The pain in my eyes was nothing compared to the pain in my heart. I ground grain like a beast for . . . actually, I don't know how long I was down there . . . without my sight, I lost all awareness of day and night. All I did was walk around and around and around the same circle. All I could think of was that God had chosen me. God had said I would be the one who would set Israel free. And now I would never do it. I would never be able to fulfill God's calling for my life. Never be able to fulfill God's mission; never be able to do the ministry he had called me to. It was all gone. And I could never get it back.

The Philistines decided to celebrate my humiliation. They sent invitations to the "who's who" to come and cut loose in the temple of Dagon, their heathen god. Everyone who was anyone came to celebrate Dagon's greatness because the champion of the God of Israel had been defeated. I was brought out for sport. To amuse the masses. They sent a servant boy to come get me. At one time I had taken on thousands of their soldiers, but now they could control me with just a boy.

As the child led me into the temple, the place erupted with laughter. This was hilarious! The hall erupted with blasphemy against God. What hurt my heart so much was that I was the one who had allowed this to happen. I couldn't blame anyone. I couldn't blame God. I couldn't blame my parents. I couldn't blame anything else. I was the one who knew what I should and should not do. And I was the one who had made those choices. God's name was being defamed because of me.

They led me up to the front, and I asked the boy if I could lean against something. I wasn't the man I once was. I put my hand against the pillar. As I felt it I realized that this was no ordinary post. This was a main supporting column. This was an important structural component of the whole building. I reached out my other hand and realized there was a second pillar beside me. And I prayed one last prayer. "God, I don't deserve it and I know I've missed the mark. I have failed to do what you've called me to do. But will you allow me to do something in your name? Allow me to stop the blasphemy."

Then I took the stance that I had taken so many times before and began to push. Harder and harder. As I did I felt the hair brush against the back of my neck once again. My hair had grown back in the time that I had been grinding grain. As I prayed and as I pushed, I felt for one last time the surge—the rush—the heat of God's Spirit through my body. My arms responded as they had so many times before. As I pushed, I began to hear the groaning and the creaking of that building. I began to hear screams as people became aware that something was wrong. But when I heard them cry out for Dagon to curse the God of Israel, I gave it one last push. The stone roof on top fell. We were all crushed. But I killed more enemies of Israel in my death than I did in my life.

I knew in that instant that I'd always be remembered for being a strong man, but not a great man. I would always be thought of as a failure. Why? Because I didn't accomplish God's purpose for my life. God had given me a mission, along with all the strength and ability I needed to accomplish it. But I traded it away, I squandered it away on sin. I thought that I could sin and it wouldn't affect me and my ministry. But I was wrong! I was the strongest man who ever lived. Nobody could stop me. Nobody could take anything away from me. But I gave away my ministry in exchange for the pleasures of sin.

Your ministry, what God has created you to do, will be different from what he created me to do. But I'm here to tell you, as one who has learned the hard way, that nobody can take your ministry away from you. There is no enemy so great that God is not able to preserve you and enable you to do what he has created you to do. But I'm also here to tell you that you can give your ministry away. You can allow sin to steal it. What I learned is that nobody sins and gets away with it. Not me, not even you.

The Cripple's Story

2 SAMUEL 1 – 9

DON SUNUKJIAN

(The speaker enters on crutches, looking around, peering down hallways, admiring the majestic building he's in.)

I still don't know my way around the palace. You ought to see all the rooms. And it's kind of hard to get around *(motioning toward his mangled feet).*

This is the house of David, King David. It's the finest in the land. Imported wood *(touching, caressing).* Silk tapestries *(motioning).*

(The speaker seats himself on a piano bench.)

My name is Mephibosheth. I live here. My wife and I and our small son have a suite of rooms on the second floor. We've been here about three months now.

Why do I live here? That's a good question.

I'm not a visiting dignitary; I'm not an ambassador assigned to this country or anything like that. I'm not a court official; I have no administrative functions here. I'm not a relative either, though I admit David treats me like a son and has become a grandfather to my boy, Micah.

Why do I live here? I will tell you, for it's an amazing story.

My father was killed when I was very young. My memories are vague, for I was five years old. I remember playing in front of the house on my father's estate when a horseman came riding into the yard. I remember the furious beat of hooves, the lather on the horse, the shout from the rider to my babysitter in the house: "Take the boy and run. The Philistines are coming! The king and the prince are dead. Israel is defeated and every man is fleeing!" And then he was off to warn others.

I remember the babysitter giving a cry, grabbing her shawl, a little bit of bread and cheese, and grabbing me by the hand—"We must run! Hurry! Fast! We must run!"

We left everything on the spot, and we ran. From the sound of things, the Philistines were barely a mile away. I remember the war shouts as they overran one estate after another. We heard the sounds of futile resistance by the owners, and then men screaming as they died.

We ran and we ran. We ran all that afternoon and into the night. When it was dark, we slipped into a field to catch our breath and hopefully to sleep. But the

Philistines continued to pillage into the night, and the sounds came close again. So we got up to run once more.

We ran in the darkness—I don't know how long. We were trying to reach the river to cross over into a corner province in the north, where we did not think they would follow.

But I couldn't go on—my side ached, my lungs were bursting. I remember falling to the ground.

The babysitter said, "Come."

"I can't."

"They will kill us."

"I can't," and I started to cry.

She picked me up and began to carry me as she ran. But I was pretty big; five-year-olds can be a heavy load to carry. For a while her fear gave her strength, but as the night wore on, I noticed her eyes began to glaze with exhaustion. Her steps began to stagger. And suddenly, without warning, she collapsed.

I don't remember exactly . . . but I remember her pitching forward, with me in her arms. I remember my legs beneath me *(bending forward)* and her heavy weight falling on me, and then I remember—*(two snaps of the fingers to indicate breaking bones)*!

Something was broken! I screamed. I screamed for her to get off me, but she wasn't moving. I cried and struggled, and eventually got out from under her. I remember screaming into the night for someone to come—and then I remember nothing else.

Several days later I awoke in the house of a man named Makir, who lived far on the other side of the river we were trying to reach. I learned we had been found the next morning by others who were fleeing. They had taken us with them the next couple of days and had brought us across the river and into safety.

I must have been in shock from the pain, for I remember nothing of all that. I only know that when I woke, my ankles and feet were mangled and numb . . . and I knew that I would never walk again.

That tells you how I got to be this way. But that doesn't tell you who I am.

My father who was killed in that battle was not an ordinary soldier. He was Prince Jonathan. King Saul was my grandfather. In the course of time, if all had gone well, I would have been king of this land after my father, Jonathan.

But after the battle, all was in chaos. King Saul was dead. My father was dead. Two of my father's brothers, my uncles, were dead. The Philistines controlled our land and were seizing everything for themselves.

It took a few weeks before we could assess the situation, before the remnant of Israel's government began to appear in exile. It came together by bits and pieces, and it wasn't much.

One of my uncles had survived—Ishbosheth *(shakes head)*. Out of the strength and grandeur of Saul's house, out of the glorious manhood of Jonathan and my uncles, who should survive—Ishbosheth, the most incompetent! He had neither the heart nor the head to rule. Left to himself, he was all right, but in a position where he was expected to lead, he couldn't do it.

Fortunately, Abner also lived and made it across the river. Abner was the commander of the army, a bull of a man—strong, stalwart, muscular, and a leader—ready mind, strength of will, a man who could give orders.

For all practical purposes Abner took over the government in exile. Ishbosheth was the figurehead. Abner was loyal to him and served him as he served my grandfather. But essentially Abner was the power, the one who made things happen.

Those were difficult days, but I was not too involved. I was a boy. I was crippled. And it was obvious that whatever course the kingdom took, it would take it without me. I was shunted aside; I was not to have any part of the kingship.

Well, that soon became of no matter, for it was not long before the kingship was gone from our family. For, after seven years, when I was twelve, the whole land turned from us to David.

And that's the way it's been for the fifteen years since then—David.

How did David and I get together?

I had never met David until three months ago when we moved here.

My early opinion before I knew him was bitter. From what I'd been told, he and my father Jonathan knew each other once. When they were young, they were best friends. They fought side by side. But something must have happened, for by the time I was born, David was an outlaw and considered a traitor.

There were two explanations for this. Some said that my grandfather King Saul had an insane jealousy of David and had tried to kill him—that he had an irrational hatred of David and that David had had to flee to protect himself.

Others said my grandfather saw through David and knew that beneath the surface, David was treacherously scheming to take the kingship for himself and away from my father, Jonathan.

I was inclined to believe the latter explanation—that David was a scheming traitor—for a couple of reasons. One, at the time of the battle in which my father was killed, David was living with the enemy in Philistia. According to reports he had even volunteered to help the Philistines in the battle, but was turned down. Two, soon after the battle and Israel's defeat, while we were trying to regroup in the north, David moved back into the southern section of our land and had himself crowned king of the southern tribes.

So my early opinion of him was negative. And this opinion seemed to be confirmed seven years later when I was twelve. At that time Abner, our leader, had gone south to negotiate a consolidation of our northern part of the kingdom with David's southern part. While there he was tricked into a secret meeting and killed by one of David's generals. A few days later Ishbosheth was assassinated in the north.

I heard the assassins were executed by David, but who knows whether this was genuine justice or whether David was simply silencing his henchmen after they had done his dirty work. "Dead men tell no tales," you know.

In either case, with Abner and Ishbosheth dead, David became king of all the land, and that's the way it's been for the last fifteen years.

And I have to admit, regardless of what I thought about David, it's been good for the kingdom. There's been a great expansion of territory, an unbroken string of victories, stability, prosperity. There's even been talk of a dynasty, a dynasty founded by David. Supposedly David has had a dream in which God promised that David's sons would rule after him—a dynasty. And there's even a promise of some Great Son in the future.

During all these events I was left in that far northern province, apparently forgotten. Makir was kind—I married his daughter, we had a small son. I did what I could to make myself useful—some bookkeeping for Makir, a little carpentry. I'm not good, but I appreciate fine wood *(glances around palace)*.

And that brings me up to about three months ago, which is when it happened. One day Ziba showed up with the message: "David wants to see you."

I hadn't seen Ziba for about ten years. Ziba used to manage the estate for my father and grandfather. He too had fled across the river, but he had returned when things stabilized under David. He was living near our old home area, and from what I had heard, he was doing OK for himself.

He said, "David wants to see you." That sounded ominous. Why does David want to see me? *(Light dawns!)* He's going to kill me! To establish a dynasty requires the elimination of all rivals. I'm the last living member of Saul's line. With Jonathan, my uncles, and Ishbosheth dead, I'm the last one who could make a claim to the throne and take the lost inheritance. By getting rid of me, the last potential enemy, David makes his dynasty secure.

I didn't want to see David, but the wagon was waiting to take me there. I had no choice. I could have asked for Makir to help, but that simply would have brought retaliation against him for interfering. I kissed my wife good-bye. Neither of us thought we would see the other again.

On the way there in the wagon I asked Ziba, "How did David hear about me?"

"One day he sent word for me to come to the palace. When I got there, he asked if any of Jonathan's descendants were still living. I told him about you."

"Why? Why not keep your mouth shut?"

"Because I was afraid he'd find out anyway and then punish me for not telling him. Besides, he said his intentions toward you were good."

"Fool! What possible reason could he have for doing good to me? He has everything to gain by my death. . . . I'm going to my execution."

We rode in silence until we came to Jerusalem. *(Gaping awe!)* I had heard about the new capital David had built, but this was unbelievable. What an impregnable fortress! And the palace—never had I seen such a place!

I was taken inside and told to "sit here" in some waiting room while Ziba went through some doors. He came back in just a few minutes and directed me through the doors.

I went through the doors into a great room. At the other end, someone was sitting. It was obviously David. As I hobbled toward him, he watched me in silence, with penetrating gaze.

I thought, "He's going to kill me. I'm a threat to his kingdom, to the stability of his dynasty. But if he's going to kill me, I'm going to make it as hard on him as I can. I'm not going to give him the satisfaction of appearing rebellious."

So with great difficulty *(kneeling)* I got on my knees and bowed to indicate that he was my king.

I heard a thunderous voice: "Mephibosheth!"

With my head still bowed, I said, "I am your loyal servant."

Then I heard, "Don't be afraid."

I looked up . . . his eyes were smiling and his face seemed kind. He told me, "Rise, and sit by me on the seat."

"Your father," he continued, "was my dearest friend. When we were young, we both knew that the kingship would be taken from Saul's house, and that I was to rule. At that time your father made me swear that when this happened, I would never harm him. He made me vow that as God blessed me and I was established as king, I would never raise my hand against any of his descendants.

"Thirty years ago I made a covenant with your father, a solemn promise, that when that time came, I would act kindly to any of his descendants.

"I have sought you out and brought you here in order to fulfill my promise. I am restoring to you all of the land and estate of your father and grandfather. The farmlands, the cattle, the orchards, the buildings—they are all yours. All the revenues that the estate produces are yours. All of its operations are in your hands. Ziba will return to your service as foreman, just as he was for your father and grandfather. His sons and servants will work the land and turn over the revenues to you.

"You will have an entirely free hand. You may come and go as you please, for whatever your business requires. But I want you to bring your wife and boy here to the palace and be part of my family."

That was three months ago. Today I am a wealthy man and a member of David's family. Here was a king who owed me nothing. But he determined to seek me out and lift me up.

What was I to him? I could offer him nothing. In fact, in his eyes, I was a potential enemy. I was hostile to his rule.

But he brought me to his palace, restored the inheritance I had lost, and made me part of his family. And I have shared the laughter and love of his house ever since.

I've got to go now. Thank you for letting me tell my story.

(Gets up and exits, slowly pausing every few steps to say another of the following sentences.)

You know that dream David had—where sons of his sons would rule, until there comes some "Great Son of David"? I wonder if there will ever be a "Son of David" who will be anything like his father? *(Steps)*

Do you think there will ever be a Son of David who will seek out an enemy and lift him up, who will restore the inheritance that was lost? *(Steps)*

Would he take a cripple and make him a son of the king?

If he would, I hope you get to meet him.

(Exit)

Mary of Bethany

MARK 14:1 – 11

ALICE MATHEWS

(Alice Mathews as herself)

Matthew, Mark, and John all record a lovely event that took place just a few days before Jesus' crucifixion. If we take these three gospel accounts together, we can see details we might miss if we read only one gospel account. Let me help you see this event through the eyes of someone who was there . . .

(Alice Mathews in character)

Have you ever been misunderstood—when from the depths of your soul, you wanted to do something for God—something costly, or difficult, but wonderful? But folks around you didn't understand? They thought you were crazy or foolish or wasteful? If you've ever had that experience, you'll understand my story.

My name is Mary. I live with my sister Martha and my brother Lazarus in the village of Bethany. We're just two miles east of our capital city, Jerusalem. It's nice to be so close to our temple there. We can easily take part in all of our national feasts. Perhaps that's why Jesus and those who traveled with him came to Bethany often to stay during the festivals. And whenever they came, we always welcomed Jesus and his followers into our home.

Whenever we'd hear that Jesus was climbing the hill to our village, my sister Martha would hurry around the house, fixing a comfortable place for Jesus to sit as he taught us the Scriptures and the way to God. And do you know what? He'd even let *me*, a woman, sit at his feet and listen to him teach! Other rabbis wouldn't soil their reputations by teaching women, but not Jesus. He was different.

In fact, one time when my sister Martha interrupted his teaching to ask him to make me help her in the kitchen, he told her that I had chosen the good part, and it wouldn't be taken away from me. Can you imagine that? He not only let me listen. He encouraged me to learn at his feet. No one had ever, ever done that for me before.

Then there was the time when our brother Lazarus got sick. We knew that he was very sick, so we sent word to Jesus to come quickly and heal him. We had seen him heal others and we knew he could heal any disease. But he didn't come to us—and Lazarus died. I don't think I've ever felt more let down in my life. Then four days after the funeral, Jesus arrived. I fell at his feet and sobbed and sobbed: "Lord, if you had just been here, my brother would not have died!" I knew Jesus could have healed Lazarus if only he had gotten to Bethany earlier.

Jesus didn't answer me, but he turned to some of the villagers standing nearby and asked where Lazarus had been buried. So we led him to the cave on the side of the hill. Then he said, "Take away the stone at the entrance."

But Martha—my practical sister!—said, "Lord, no! By now there's a terrible stench because he's been dead for four days."

But Jesus told her, "Martha, didn't I just tell you that if you would believe, you would see the glory of God?"

So Martha motioned to some men to remove the stone. Then, after praying to God in front of us all, Jesus called in a loud voice, "Lazarus, come forth!" And before our very eyes, our brother came staggering out of that cave, still wrapped hand and foot in the grave clothes.

I hardly have to tell you, that was the most extraordinary moment in my life! My brother—who had been *dead*—was once again with us, alive and well! Jesus could even raise the dead to life again! How could anyone fail to believe that he is God's Messiah? Before that moment Jesus had been my wonderful Teacher, but now he was so much more. He was the Christ, the Son of God, my Savior. The more I thought about this, the more I wanted to show him how much I loved him. I wanted to do something very special for him. But what?

Six days before Passover, Jesus came back to Bethany. We were overjoyed! Simon the leper invited Jesus to a dinner at his house, and my sister Martha oversaw the preparation of all of the food. Brother Lazarus was one of the invited guests. And suddenly, I knew what I wanted to do for Jesus!

I hurried back to our home and opened the small chest in the corner of the room. There it was, the small alabaster flask that I had guarded for many years. It contained the most expensive perfume money can buy—a pint of oil of spikenard. It would take an average person a full year to earn enough money to buy this flask and its contents. Cradling the flask carefully in my hands, I hurried back to Simon's house.

Dinner had begun. There were Jesus and Lazarus and the other guests reclining on couches around Simon's dinner table. I crossed the room quietly and stood behind Jesus. Then I raised the alabaster flask over Jesus' head, snapped off the neck of the bottle, and began pouring the fragrant perfumed oil on his head. Then I knelt at his feet and continued pouring out the costly oil over his ankles, down between his toes. With no towel nearby, I reached up and released my long hair and used it to wipe Jesus' feet. I was so engulfed in my love for Jesus and my delight in pouring this expensive perfume over his head and feet that I hardly noticed anyone else in the room.

And then suddenly I heard them—the indignant voices. One of Jesus' followers—it was Judas—asked, "Why was this fragrant oil wasted? It could have been sold for more than 300 denarii and given to the poor!" Then the others chimed in: "Yes, why? That was a stupid thing to do! What a waste!"

I looked at the faces around the table: no smiles, only frowns. The air was rich with the fragrance, but no one seemed to enjoy it. What had seemed to me to be such a good idea seemed stupid or thoughtless or selfish to the others in the room. I heard the cutting words. I saw the scowls. What had happened? What had I done? Was I wrong?

Judas and the others could be right. What he said was logical; the perfume could have been sold and the money given to the poor. That made sense.

Had I really wasted something that would better have served others in need? I knew that what I did was extravagant. But was it evil?

In this one lavish gesture of love for Jesus, had I made a terrible mistake?

I had heard his concern for the poor. After all the hours I had listened to Jesus teach, had I missed the point of his life and his ministry?

I was still kneeling at Jesus' feet with the empty flask in my hand when I heard Jesus speak. He said to them, "Leave her alone! Why are you bothering her? She has done a beautiful thing for me. The poor you will always have with you, and you can help them any time you want. But you will not always have me. She did what she could. She poured perfume on my body beforehand to prepare for my burial. I tell you the truth, wherever the gospel is preached throughout the world, what she has done will also be told, in memory of her."

Were my ears deceiving me? Jesus just said that I had done a *beautiful* thing for him! *He* knew that I loved him and wanted to show him my love. And he said it was beautiful.

But Jesus said more. He also said that what I had done was so beautiful that not only would he never forget it, but he wouldn't let the world forget it. Wherever his story is told, my story would also be told.

I looked at Jesus as he spoke these words. They were medicine for my soul. I knew as I looked into his eyes that he was pleased. To others at the table what I had done seemed extravagant and wasteful. But to Jesus? He put a different value on my gift. He understood my heart. He recognized my love.

In that moment, I knew that there are acts of worship that the understanding cannot understand. Love has its reasons that reason knows not of. But Jesus saw. He knew. And he understood.

(Alice Mathews as herself)

There is a devotion we can have to Jesus Christ that is conventional and acceptable to others. It stays within the boundaries of conformity. But Mary's response to Jesus went beyond conventional boundaries. She saw him with new eyes. He was more than a great rabbi or a great healer. He was the resurrection and the life. And that vision of Jesus drew from her abandoned worship, a devotion that went far beyond conventional boundaries.

When people really see a life poured out for Christ, they never full appreciate it. It looks like fanaticism or waste. But Jesus knows our hearts and values the gift of ourselves as we pour out our lives at his feet. And when we truly know him as the resurrection and the life, we are moved to give him all that we are, all that we have.

IMPLEMENTATION WORKSHEETS

Understanding Narrative Literature

Worksheet Summarizing Steps in the Exegetical Task

(CORRESPONDS TO CHAPTERS 2, 3, 4)

1. Adjust your interpretive paradigm.

   - Biblical narratives are more than just history. They are theology. Their primary purpose is to reveal God and how we should live in response to him.
   - Your exegetical goal is not just to discover information about the story you want to preach. Your primary objective is to determine how the original author utilized the details of the story to communicate a primary idea to the original audience. Keep your eye on the prize. Your goal is intent, not just content!
   - These stories rank among the finest literature ever written. They are not poorly stitched together myths. Every detail is intentional and significant.

2. Understand the larger context of your story.

   a. Read the entire book through a few times.

   b. When was the book written?
      - What is happening with the people of God at this time?

      _____

      - How does this book contribute to the timeline of biblical history?

      _____

      - What was happening in the broader historical context?

      _____

   c. Who was the target audience of this book? (The stories of Scripture were not written for the people in the story.)

      _____

d. Why did the original author write this book?
  • What contemporary challenge motivated the original author?

  _____

  • What subject is being addressed?

  _____

3. Determine the structure of your story.

  a. Examine the individual scenes of the story (use the Scene Analysis Chart to guide you).

  b. Determine where the story begins and ends.
    • What is the primary source of tension in this particular story? Write it down.

    _____

    • How do the scenes contribute to the tension of the story? Observe how the author gradually increases the tension of the story to the point of climax and then achieves final resolution. (The mono-mythic cycle is helpful.)

    _____

    _____

    _____

    • Where is the "unexpected twist" in the plot? (Does this twist fully dissipate the tension?)

    _____

    _____

    • Where do you think the story ends? Does this story have a happy ending, or is it a tragedy? Why?

    _____

    _____

    _____

    • Are there any obvious literary markers that mark the beginning and end of this particular story?

    _____

- *Helpful hints*
  - Irony and poetic justice can confirm your understanding of the plot. If either is present in your story, they should be most visible in the "unexpected twist" of the plot.
  - Repetition can also confirm your understanding of the plot. Narrators sometimes repeat themselves to highlight their "big idea." Do words or events recur?

  _____

  - Narrators will occasionally intertwine the plots of two related stories to communicate a single big idea. Is that happening here?

  _____

  - Narrators slow the story down for emphasis. Where does the story slow down?

  _____

  - Narrators occasionally dischronologize events. Are the events presented in a different order than they occurred historically?

  _____

4. Analyze the characters (refer to Character Analysis Sheet).

   a. Write down the names of every character on the Character Analysis sheet.

   b. What does the biblical text reveal about these characters?

   c. Is there any contrast, comparison, physical appearance, commonplace references, repetition?

   d. Identify the literary role occupied by each character (protagonist, antagonist, or foil).

   e. In-depth character analysis
      - Motivation (why did they act this way?)
      - Identification (how am I similar to them?)

5. Discover the setting of the story.

   a. Geography.
      - Where is your story situated geographically?

   _____

- Does this influence the story?

  _____

- Is the story affected in any way by the topography of the area?

  _____

b. Culture. Are there any social practices of that day that inform the story?

  _____

  _____

6. State the "big idea" of the narrative.

What does the text say? Crystallize what you have learned. Synthesize the author's central idea out of what you have discovered. Clearly state what the original author intended to communicate to the original recipients of this story. Go beyond content to intent.

a. Exegetical idea
- Locate the unexpected twist in the plot.
- What is the subject/topic that is being resolved here?
- Does the author want you to emulate or avoid the protagonist's choice?
- Summarize your understanding of what happened in this story in the form of a subject and complement. Make sure that your subject is written in the form of a question, and that your complement is the full and complete answer to that question. Be as accurate and literal as possible. (Hint: it should include the names of dead people!)

  – Subject

    _____

  – Complement

    _____

b. Homiletical idea
This is the same idea you wrote above, but rewritten in eternal terms. This idea will not contain the names of dead people. While it will be essentially the same as the exegetical idea, it will be understandable and applicable to a twenty-first-century audience.

  – Subject

    _____

– Complement

_____

c. Preaching idea

This is a short, pithy, memorable phrase that will lodge in the minds of your audience. It will not be as comprehensive as your exegetical or homiletical ideas. But it will nail those ideas deep into the lives of your listeners.

7. Double check your big idea.

- Does your idea make sense out of every part of the story?

_____

- Does the big idea fit easily into the context?

_____

- Does it fit through the filter of systematic theology?

_____

- Does it have an explosive force to it?

_____

8. Application. What does the text mean?

a. What is the central principle espoused in this passage?

_____

b. What would this story look like if it were updated to the twenty-first century?

_____

c. In what way would your life (and those who will hear this message) change if you learned and applied the lesson of this story?

_____

d. In what way would your life (and those who will hear this message) change if the lesson of this story were ignored?

_____

Scene Analysis Chart

Passage	
Exegetical observations	
Summary What happened? Recap the activity of this scene in one sentence.	
Dramatic purpose • What did this scene accomplish for the overall story? • Is the tension increasing or decreasing? • How did the author manipulate the tension?	

Character Identification Sheet

Characters (*Who* is part of this story?)	
Descriptions (What *kind* of people are they? What do you know about them?)	
Actions (What did the characters *do*?)	
Motivation (Why did the characters act this way?)	
Emotion (How do the characters *feel* as the events occurred?)	

Scene Development Chart

Scene #	
Action summary (What happens? State in one sentence what you want to occur in this scene.)	
Dramatic purpose (How will this scene modify the tension of the story to advance the plot?)	
Character activity (What did the characters say and do in this scene?)	

Developing a First-Person Sermon

Worksheet Summarizing Steps in the Homiletical Task
(BASED ON CHAPTERS 5-6)

1. Select the text: What passage do you intend to preach?

   _____

   a. Is this a natural unit of Scripture? Be sure you selected a *whole* story and not just a fragment.

   b. Is this an emotionally charged or action-packed story?

2. Understand the text.

   a. What is the surprising twist in the plot?

   _____

   b. Exegetical idea: What happened in the story?

      ✎ Subject: _____

      ✎ Complement: _____

   c. Homiletical idea: What does the story mean today?

      ✎ Subject: _____

      ✎ Complement: _____

   d. Preaching idea (memorable "bumper sticker" phrase):

   _____

3. Develop your protagonist (main character).

   a. What individual will *best* reveal the main idea of the biblical text (biblical or imaginary)?

   _____

    ✍ Will this person live out or be extremely close to the action & unexpected twist?

    ✍ Are you the same gender as the protagonist?

b. Give the protagonist a dominant defining characteristic.

_____

c. Get to know your protagonist as well as their mother did. On separate sheets of paper sketch out the particulars of your protagonist's life. Be sure to include:

    ✍ Background (home life, urban/rural, socioeconomic status, education, formative childhood influences)

    ✍ Physical characteristics (race, age, strength, carriage, health, speech, dress)

    ✍ Mental characteristics (native intelligence, originality, ability to learn)

    ✍ Emotional characteristics (attitude toward life, basic likes/dislikes, capacity for deep feeling, capacity to cope with crisis/change in environment)

    ✍ Spiritual/moral characteristics (level of faith and ethical development, inner motivations, spiritual qualities, relationship with God)

    ✍ Identify the vital traits.

d. Personal identification. How are you and your listeners similar to this character?

_____

_____

_____

4. Develop your antagonist.

    On separate sheets of paper, describe your antagonist. This description should be written in similar detail. Be sure, however, that your antagonist:

a. Is more powerful than the protagonist.

b. Has an understandable motivation.

c. Is strong where the protagonist is weak.

5. Set the story. Where does this story take place? What is its:

a. Period—time of story

_____

b. Duration—length of story

_____

   c. Location—geography of story

_____

_____

6. Plot the action.

   a. Start at the climax / twist of the story.

On a blank piece of paper draw a large mono-mythic circle. At the very bottom of the circle, write the unexpected event that twisted the plot of the biblical narrative. This will be the surprising twist of your sermon.

As you look at the left side of the circle, think about what scenes will be necessary to take your sermon from summer to this twist.

   b. How will you need to modify the ancient story for a modern audience?
- ✍ New characters?
- ✍ New or merged scenes?
- ✍ Rearranged scenes?

   c. Increase conflict and tension.
- ✍ Reverse the big idea.

Anti-subject:

_____

Anti-complement:

_____

- ✍ View the big idea like a skeptic. How would the sharpest critic you know criticize the big idea of the biblical narrative?

_____

_____

_____

   d. Avoid common mistakes.
- ✍ Start with inciting event.
- ✍ Choose action over soliloquy.

   e. Double-check your structure.
- ✍ Did you just rerun the story?
- ✍ Is the climax the same as the biblical story?
- ✍ Does your protagonist have character arc?

7. Determine the perspective.

   a. Will your character invite listeners to go back in their imagination to the ancient life and times of the original events?

   b. Will your character emerge out of the past to speak to the contemporary audience?

   c. Will your character involve the audience as current participants in the historical past?

8. Create lesser characters—the fewer the better and only for dramatic effect.

9. Write the manuscript.

   a. Start with the unexpected twist.

   b. Go to the beginning and start with the inciting event.

10. Decide about props.

    a. Will the object embody the big idea of the text?

    b. Will it add or distract from your message?

    c. Is it culturally appropriate?

11. Refine your manuscript.
    ✍ Read it aloud.
    ✍ Use your body.

12. Block your sermon.
    ✍ Experienced preachers can match the content of the sermon with the appropriate platform location.

13. Rehearse your sermon.
    ✍ Rehearse 2–5 times with notes and 2–5 times without notes.

14. Decide about costuming.
    ✍ Go ahead if you can do it with excellence and it strengthens your sermon.

15. Deliver your sermon.
    ✍ Say the words.
    ✍ Become the person.

SCRIPTURE INDEX

SUBJECT INDEX

We want to hear from you. Please send your comments about this book to us in care of zreview@zondervan.com. Thank you.

ZONDERVAN™

GRAND RAPIDS, MICHIGAN 49530 USA

WWW.ZONDERVAN.COM